Minority Shareholders' Remedies

A. J. Boyle assesses the current state of English company law on minority shareholders' remedies from historical, theoretical and comparative perspectives in this important new addition to *Cambridge Studies in Corporate Law*.

He analyses the reforms of the UK Law Commission, which have been further appraised and amplified by the work in progress of the Company Law Review Steering Group. The book covers the common law actions by exception to the rule in *Foss* v. *Harbottle*, and the statutory remedies by way of petition for unfair prejudice and/or just and equitable winding up. As well as considering the complexities of derivative actions and statutory minority remedies, Boyle discusses future directions for minority shareholders' remedies.

This book will be of interest to academics and practitioners in company and corporate law, particularly in the UK, USA, France and Germany, as well as throughout the Commonwealth.

A. J. BOYLE is Emeritus Professor of Law in the University of London. He is General Editor of *Gore-Browne on Companies* (1972 to date) and original joint author of *Boyle and Bird's Company Law* (four editions, 1982–2000). He has published widely in the field of company law.

Cambridge Studies in Corporate Law

Series Editor
Professor Barry Rider,
University of London

Corporate or company law encompasses the law relating to the creation, operation and management of corporations and their relationships with other legal persons. *Cambridge Studies in Corporate Law* is a major new initiative offering an academic platform for discussion of these issues. The series is international in its choice of both authors and subjects, and aims to publish the best original scholarship on topics ranging from labour law to financial and capital regulation.

Minority shareholders' remedies

A. J. Boyle

CAMBRIDGE
UNIVERSITY PRESS

PUBLISHED BY THE PRESS SYNDICATE OF THE UNIVERSITY OF CAMBRIDGE
The Pitt Building, Trumpington Street, Cambridge, United Kingdom

CAMBRIDGE UNIVERSITY PRESS
The Edinburgh Building, Cambridge CB2 2RU, UK
40 West 20th Street, New York NY 10011–4211, USA
477 Williamstown Road, Port Melbourne, VIC 3207, Australia
Ruiz de Alarcón 13, 28014 Madrid, Spain
Dock House, The Waterfront, Cape Town 8001, South Africa

http://www.cambridge.org

© A. J. Boyle 2002

First published 2002

Printed in the United Kingdom at the University Press, Cambridge

Typeface Plantin 10/12 pt.   *System* LATEX 2$_\varepsilon$ [TB]

A catalogue record for this book is available from the British Library.

Library of Congress Cataloguing in Publication Data

Boyle, A. J.
Minority shareholders' remedies / A. J. Boyle.
    p.   cm. – (Cambridge studies in corporate law)
Includes bibliographical references and index.
ISBN 0 521 79106 5 (hbk.)
1. Stockholders' derivative actions – Great Britain.   2. Minority stockholders –
Legal status, laws, etc. – Great Britain.   3. Remedies (Law) – Great Britain.
I. Title.   II. Series.
KD2100 .B69   2002
346.41'0666 – dc21   2001043260

ISBN 0 521 79106 5 hardback

Contents

Preface

It must be admitted that there is already an extensive literature in the form of both monographs and periodical articles on the subject of minority remedies. A further attempt to explore this controversial and complex subject is nevertheless warranted not only by the continuing developments in the case law but even more so by the fundamental reforming work of the Law Commission, as further appraised and amplified by the work in progress of the Company Law Review Steering Group. To this must be added the impact of the new Civil Procedure Rules and the possible effect of conditional fee agreements.

The first two chapters explore in turn the *Foss* v. *Harbottle* rule and the common law actions that the rule itself permits despite its general prohibition against minority suits. These topics are explored in the context of their legal history as well as in the light of legal theory and comparative law. Consideration is given to the possible reasons for the long neglect of this area by law reformers. A further matter requiring attention relates to the problems in terms of both policy and practice posed by the public listed company.

The most significant reform set out in the Law Commission's Report on shareholder remedies is a new statutory derivative action to replace its common law equivalent. Broadly, this new remedy is based on models provided by existing Commonwealth legislation. The Law Commission's version is, however, somewhat more cautiously conservative than, for example, the well-tested Canadian model. The Law Commission's proposed remedy if not further amended will provide little overall improvement on the common law derivative action in the case of public listed companies. It is here that a more effective new remedy is most needed. For private companies, the existing minority remedies are largely adequate.

The last two chapters are devoted to the linked statutory remedies by way of petition on the ground of unfair prejudice and/or for just and equitable winding up. A significant development here is the House of Lords' endeavour to set out a new conceptual framework for the ever expanding case law on unfair prejudice. Academic scholarship has also had a useful part to play in theorising the unfair prejudice remedy. The Law Commission's attempt to frame an expeditious and simplified procedure applicable to owner-managed companies deserves more attention than it has yet received. The Company Law Review Steering Group has been much too dismissive of the Law Commission's work in this respect. This study of minority shareholders' remedies makes two assumptions. First of all, it is assumed that the specialised procedures allowing minority shareholders to apply to court in particular statutory contexts (e.g. mergers or takeovers or constitutional amendments) lie beyond the scope the present study. Secondly, it assumed that the readers of this monograph have a sound understanding of company law in general and directors' duties in particular.

Table of cases

Table of statutes

1   The rule in *Foss* v. *Harbottle*

Introduction

This chapter is concerned with the rule in *Foss* v. *Harbottle*.[1] The chapter explores the historical origins and subsequent evolution of a rule whose principal effect is to bar minority shareholders' actions. The treatment of minority actions by exception to the rule, or lying beyond its scope, is the subject-matter of Chapter 2. Chapter 3 is concerned with a proposed statutory derivative action. This is intended to reform defects in the common law shareholder's derivative action.

Inevitably, as part of the process of exploring the conceptual thinking on which the rule in *Foss* v. *Harbottle* rests, as well as the judicial policies it expresses, this chapter will begin to open up some of the themes[2] that will be explored more fully in Chapters 2 and 3. Chapter 1 also explores the slow process of reforming the rule and the factors which appear to have inhibited both the judiciary and the Department of Trade and Industry in undertaking that task of reform. The particular difficulties that beset the use of the derivative action against directors and other wrongdoers in public listed companies are also considered in Chapter 1.[3]

Relying on certain judicial decisions and *dicta* early in the last century, some academic writers have put forward a seemingly attractive solution to the problems posed by the rule in *Foss* v. *Harbottle*. This takes the form of invoking the provisions of the membership contract contained in what is now section 14 of the Companies Act 1985. The question this theory raises is how far it can be reconciled, if at all, with the general body of case law associated with the rule in *Foss* v. *Harbottle*.

This chapter concludes with a review of some reflections found in the writing of corporate law theorists on the significance of shareholder

---

[1] (1843) 2 Hare 461.

[2] E.g. 'fraud on a minority' and 'wrongdoer control'. Cross-references in the footnotes indicate where further examination occurs.

[3] This is an important issue that goes to the heart of the matter in determining the role of shareholders' actions as a mode of civil redress in policing corporate abuse. This issue is further explored in Chapters 2 and 3.

litigation in the general system of corporate governance.[4] In Chapter 2, the shareholders' action will be examined in the context of American and European law.

The origins of the English rule in *Foss* v. *Harbottle*

The origin of what is now known in English law as the rule in *Foss* v. *Harbottle*[5] can be traced to some early-nineteenth-century decisions in the law of partnership. In the previous century, it had been established that the Chancellor would not interfere in the internal disputes of a partnership 'except with a view to a dissolution'. Since harmony between partners is not to be had by decree, equity would not act in vain. In the early nineteenth century, however, the Chancellors relented from their previous refusal to intervene except with a view to dissolution. The old rule was restated in a form better adapted to the needs of the increasing number of unincorporated joint stock companies. Now it was only in the case of 'matters of internal regulation' that the Chancellor would refuse to act except with a view to dissolution.[6]

In one of the earliest of these cases, *Carlen* v. *Drury*,[7] the Chancellor declined to interfere because the articles of 'partnership' provided a very effective internal remedy for mismanagement. Under these articles the general meeting had annually to appoint a committee of twelve, which had the power to report to a subsequent general meeting called by them on any misbehaviour by the managers. The plaintiff members had made no attempt to seek redress in this way, but Lord Eldon made it clear that the 'refusal or neglect of the committee to act' in a case of delinquency 'clearly made out' might raise a case 'for prompt and immediate interference'.[8] It should be noted that as yet no mention is made of the principle of majority rule. Lord Eldon simply declined to intervene 'before the parties have tried that jurisdiction which the articles themselves have provided'.

---

[4] The English theoretical literature in respect of the unfair prejudice petition is examined in Chapter 4.

[5] See Boyle, (1975) 28 *Modern Law Review* 317 at 318–20; and Wedderburn, (1957) *Cambridge Law Journal* 194 at 196–8. For a general account of the origins and development of English company law, see P. L. Davies (ed.), *Gower's Principles of Modern Company Law* (6th ed., London, Sweet & Maxwell, 1997), Chapters 2 and 3.

[6] This rule, and the *Foss* v. *Harbottle* rule which grew out of it, were entirely creations of the Chancellor. The Chancellor had acquired almost exclusive jurisdiction over internal disputes in partnerships and companies. In the case of companies, this jurisdiction was originally founded upon the trust created by the deed of settlement and, at a later date, upon the remedies sought and the fiduciary duties of the directors.

[7] (1812) V & B 154. See also *Waters* v. *Taylor* (1807) 15 Ves 10; *Ellison* v. *Bignold* (1821) 2 Jac & W 503 at 511.

[8] (1812) V & B 154 at 159.

Although the extent of the majority's power to ratify has not yet been explored, the majority were already conceded a right to jurisdiction over any 'internal' dispute.

It is not a matter of chance that, while the Chancellor applied a general rule of non-intervention to every type of partnership, this rule took the particular form described above only in the case of joint stock companies. In such companies, with a large and fluctuating membership, ownership was already considerably divorced from management. Shares were in practice freely transferable and an internal procedure for remedying grievances was frequently provided. In *Carlen* v. *Drury* itself, though the parties were termed 'partners in a joint concern', the articles allowed as many as 1,600 persons to become partners, and 300 of them brought the action. The social and economic character of such an undertaking was clearly very different from that of an ordinary 'private' partnership.[9] In the form in which the old rule was still applied to such partnerships it bears a far more tenuous resemblance to the *Foss* v. *Harbottle* rule as it later developed. In a 'private' partnership there was never any question of an aggrieved partner first seeking a remedy within the partnership even if he were in a minority. The Chancellors simply refused to intervene in 'partnership squabbles' or 'mere passing improprieties'.[10] However, by the early nineteenth century, the Chancellor would grant relief without insisting upon a dissolution[11] where to do so would be of advantage only to the wrongdoer.[12]

A major advance in the law in regard to minority shareholders was marked by the decision in *Foss* v. *Harbottle*[13] which transformed the old partnership rule into one of the leading principles of modern company law. Though the case concerned a statutory company created by private Act, the decision came just before Gladstone's Act of 1844 extended the right to incorporate to ordinary trading companies by simply registering their deed of settlement. The courts had now to apply a quasi-partnership rule in a corporate setting.

---

[9] It was not until many years later that the courts recognised the essential legal difference between a partnership and an unincorporated company. See James LJ in *Re Agricultural Insurance Co.* (1870) 5 Ch App 725.

[10] See, for example, *Marshall* v. *Colman* (1820) 2 J & W 266.

[11] *Smith* v. *Jeyes* (1841) 4 Beav 503.

[12] *Richards* v. *Davies* (1831) 2 Russ & M 347; and *Harrison* v. *Armitage* (1819) 3 Hare 387. On the application of the embryonic form of the *Foss* v. *Harbottle* rule, originally developed for unincorporated companies, to unincorporated associations today, see *Dawkins* v. *Antrobus* (1881) 17 ChD 615 (CA). The ordinary *Foss* v. *Harbottle* rule applies to trade unions and friendly societies. See *Edwards* v. *Halliwell* [1950] 2 All ER 1064 (CA).

[13] See (1843) 2 Hare 461 at 494–5. See further *Mozeley* v. *Alston* (1847) 1 Ph 790; and *Bailey* v. *Birkenhead Railway* (1850) 12 Beav 433 at 441.

In his judgment in *Foss* v. *Harbottle*,[14] Wigram VC followed the older cases on unincorporated companies by insisting that the minority must show that they had exhausted any possibility of redress within the internal forum. Some notion of majority rule had been implicit in the earlier cases, but Wigram VC was the first to state plainly that the court will not intervene where a majority of the shareholders may lawfully ratify irregular conduct. This is a somewhat circular argument. On the other hand, his judgment implies that where it is futile to hope for action by the general meeting a suit may nevertheless be brought by the minority even for matters which might in law be ratified by the majority. On this last point, the rule was to become even more unfavourable to the minority. It was later established that the *Foss* v. *Harbottle* rule barred a minority action whenever the alleged misconduct was in law capable of ratification, whether or not an independent majority would ever be given a real opportunity to consider the matter.[15]

Wigram VC's judgment is also notable for his discovery of an entirely new principle to support that of majority rule. For in the corporate character of the company he found a second ground for restricting minority actions. Since an incorporated company was the 'proper plaintiff' in any action concerning its rights or its constitution, it would only be very exceptionally in the case of grave abuse that a minority might be allowed to sue in their own name by joining the company as defendant. This principle, that the company itself was the proper plaintiff in proceedings concerning its rights, was closely linked with the discretion exercised by the courts of equity over the use of the representative form of action. It was to have a considerable influence upon the later Victorian judges in adopting an increasingly restrictive attitude to minority actions for breach of the articles or breach of duty by directors.

In the decade following *Foss* v. *Harbottle*, the scope of the exceptions to the rule was only vaguely indicated. The task of defining the exact extent of the exceptions to the rule was to be the work of later generations of judges. On the other hand, the more obvious implications of Wigram VC's judgment were soon to be drawn. Where, as in *Mozeley* v. *Alston*, the majority were alleged to be of the same opinion as the complaining minority, there was 'obviously nothing to prevent the company from filing a bill in its corporate character'.[16] Conversely, where the general meeting

---

[14] See (1843) 2 Hare 461 at 494–5. See further *Mozeley* v. *Alston* (1847) 1 Ph 790; and *Bailey* v. *Birkenhead Railway* (1850) 12 Beav 433 at 441.

[15] See, for example, *MacDougall* v. *Gardiner* (1875) 1 ChD 13 at 25. However, a wider view was still being taken by Jessel MR in *Russell* v. *Wakefield Waterworks* (1875) LR 20 Eq 474 at 482.

[16] (1847) 1 Ph 790 at 800. See also *Exeter & Crediton Railway Co.* v. *Butler* (1847) 5 Rail Ca 211; and *Edwards* v. *Shrewsbury Railway* (1848) 2 De G & S 537.

had already sanctioned the conduct complained of by the minority, it only remained to decide whether the majority were legally entitled to ratify that particular kind of misconduct; the court might address itself to this matter at once and would not insist on a prior application to the body of the shareholders.[17] This was the first step in a gradual process by which the English courts ceased to require that the minority's complaint be referred first to the general meeting. In other respects, however, the English rule was to become more, not less, exacting.

Judicial analysis of the rule

In some cases in the late nineteenth century and in the following century, the courts attempted to do more than apply the rule or limit its application by defining exceptions to it. It has been seen, in the historical account of its gradual evolution given above, that the genesis of *Foss* v. *Harbottle* was an equitable rule of partnership law modified to meet the needs of joint stock companies. It has been said by an Australian judge that a modern registered company 'is a hybrid growth'. It is 'a partnership which has been invested with the character of a corporation, and the rules which are applicable are partly referable to both characters'.[18] This 'hybrid growth' is reflected in the hybrid character of the *Foss* v. *Harbottle* rule itself. It consists of two complementary 'arguments' or 'grounds'. From the first[19] the courts stressed the close link between these two interrelated principles: (1) the right of the majority to bar a minority action whenever they might lawfully ratify alleged misconduct; the fact that misconduct was of a kind that was ratifiable was also a bar; and (2) the normally exclusive right of the company to sue upon a corporate cause of action.

The numerous judicial *dicta*[20] combining these two 'arguments' for the *Foss* v. *Harbottle* rule in a single statement of principle strongly suggest their interdependence. What is not clear is whether the connection between them is one of logic, or whether it is simply an association of ideas hallowed by repetition. It is only to be explained by the 'hybrid' origins of both company law and the rule in *Foss* v. *Harbottle*. In the leading case of *Edwards* v. *Halliwell*,[21] Jenkins LJ made an attempt to elucidate the precise relationship between the 'majority rule' and the 'proper plaintiff' aspects

---

[17] *Lord* v. *Copper Miners* (1848) 2 Ph 740.

[18] *Australian Coal & Shale Employers' Federation* v. *Smith* (1938) 38 SR (NWS) 48 at 53.

[19] See *Foss* v. *Harbottle* (1843) 2 Hare 461 at 491–7.

[20] See, for example, *Foss* v. *Harbottle* (1843) 2 Hare 461 at 491, 492 and 494–5; *Mozeley* v. *Alston* (1847) 1 Ph 790 at 800; *Burland* v. *Earle* [1902] AC 83 at 93; and *Pavlides* v. *Jensen* [1956] 7 Ch 565 at 579.

[21] [1950] 2 All ER 1064 at 1066.

of the rule. He contended that the will of the majority, *vis-à-vis* the minority, is to be identified with that of the company. Consequently, to say that the company is *prima facie* the proper plaintiff in actions concerning its affairs is only another way of saying that the majority, within the limits of their power to ratify, have the sole right to determine whether or not a dispute shall be brought before the courts.

The weakness of this otherwise attractive explanation is that, in the cases of breaches of duty by directors, it is not enough for the minority to show that the majority could not lawfully ratify what has been done. In order to bring themselves within the fraud on a minority exception, categorised by Jenkins LJ[22] as the only true exception to the rule, it must be further shown that the alleged wrongdoers are in control of the company.[23] Here then the notion of the company as 'the proper plaintiff' has acquired a force of its own quite independent of the majority's power to ratify. It will be seen in the following chapter[24] that as this point the *Foss* v. *Harbottle* rule is most open to criticism as being unjustifiably restrictive.

Judicial policies justifying the rule

Whatever the relationship between the 'partnership' and 'corporate' aspects of the *Foss* v. *Harbottle* rule may be at the level of conceptual analysis, as practical policy arguments in favour of the rule they are clearly not self-evident. In the latter part of the nineteenth century, some judges attempted to explain the real policies that the rule was intended to serve. In *Gray* v. *Lewis*,[25] James LJ justified the principle that any 'body corporate' is the proper plaintiff in proceedings to recover its property by pointing to the obvious danger of a multiplicity of shareholders' suits in the absence of such a rule as *Foss* v. *Harbottle*. Every member would be able to sue any director, officer or shareholder alleged to have enriched themselves at the company's 'expense'. There might be as many bills in equity as there are shareholders multiplied into the number of defendants. This situation would be aggravated where suits were discontinued at will, or dismissed with costs against plaintiff shareholders with the plaintiff shareholders unable to meet those costs.[26] An obvious objection to this line of reasoning is that a court of equity should always have been able to

---

[22] See [1950] 2 All ER at 1066–9. See also *Prudential Assurance Co. Ltd* v. *Newman Industries Ltd (No. 2)* [1982] Ch 204 at 210–11.

[23] See, for example, *Pavlides* v. *Jensen* [1956] 1 Ch 565 at 575.

[24] See Chapter 2, p. 27 below.   [25] (1873) 8 Ch App 1035 at 1051.

[26] See *La Compagnie de Mayville* v. *Whitely* [1896] 1 Ch 788 at 807; *Mozeley* v. *Alston* (1847) 1 Ph 790 at 799; and *Lord* v. *Copper Miners* (1848) 2 Ph 740.

cope with this problem by exercising its powers to stay and consolidate actions.[27]

Another argument, and one at first sight much stronger, in support of the rule is advanced by Mellish LJ in *MacDougall* v. *Gardiner*.[28] If 'something has been done irregularly, which the majority are entitled to do regularly, or if something is done illegally which the majority of the company are entitled to do legally, there can be no use having litigation about it the ultimate end of which is that a meeting is called and them ultimately the majority gets its wishes'. Doubtless it is futile to allow the minority to sue where the majority have the retrospective power, by ratifying what has been done, to nullify any decision that a court may give in favour of the minority. Granted the majority's power to ratify all but the gravest forms of abuse, this is certainly a much more compelling argument than the supposed danger of a 'multiplicity of actions'.

There are still, however, two obvious flaws in this defence of *Foss* v. *Harbottle*. First of all (as has been seen already), it fails to take account of the fact that it is not sufficient in every case to show that the misconduct then alleged is incapable of ratification. Where the minority rely upon the 'fraud on a minority exception to the rule' in bringing a derivative action, it is not sufficient to show a serious non-ratifiable breach of directors' duties; they must further prove that the wrongdoers still legally control the company. As will be seen in the next chapter,[29] it is this additional hurdle that is the aspect of the *Foss* v. *Harbottle* rule that is most open to criticism.

The second flaw is Mellish LJ's defence of *Foss* v. *Harbottle* in that the distinction he implies, between the forms of misconduct which are ratifiable and those which are not, has never been governed by entirely consistent or clearly discernible principles. It will be seen in Chapter 2[30] that nothing shows this better than the rather haphazard development of circumstances, whether true exceptions or not, where shareholders' actions are permitted.

The minority shareholder as an 'unfavoured litigant'

Professor Sealy draws a contrast with other types of litigant, for example those seeking judicial review. The latter receive, on the question of *locus standi*, a more favourable judicial acceptance than does the minority shareholder: 'Time and again he is sent away with no answer, as often as

---

[27] See now the Civil Proceeding Rules 1998, Part 3, 'The Court's Case Management Powers'. See further Chapter 2.
[28] (1875) 1 ChD 13 at 25. See also *ibid.*, p. 22 *per* James LJ.
[29] See Chapter 2, p. 27 below.   [30] See Chapter 2, pp. 51–8 below.

not with a rebuke for troubling the court.'[31] This discounts the minority shareholders' undeniable statutory and contractual status as a member who may have invested thousands or even millions. These factors are not enough in themselves to determine his standing to sue in company law and indeed for most purposes they are irrelevant.[32]

Professor Sealy draws attention to a number of sources of difficulty and confusion in the case law which reinforce the generally negative judicial attitude. He points to the muddled jurisprudence on the 'proper plaintiff' principle. There is a rather confused analysis, where a particular type of wrongdoing occurs, between what is a wrong to the company and what is a wrong to the individual.[33] In the past there has been no consistency as to what stage in the legal proceedings the *Foss* v. *Harbottle* issue should be raised and on what evidential basis the issue of *locus standi* should be resolved. Usually, it has been dealt with *in limine*, but in some cases the plaintiff was allowed a full hearing before the *Foss* v. *Harbottle* issue was resolved, even if it resulted in the minority shareholder losing.[34] Certainly, in the case of the derivative action a stricter approach is now taken. The Court of Appeal[35] has insisted that the *locus standi* point must be raised at any interlocutory stage without submission of evidence. This approach is directly linked with the characterisation of the *Foss* v. *Harbottle* rule as a purely procedural matter. As such, a less rigorous approach to providing a fully reasoned basis for a decision may result than would be the case if a principle or rule of substantive law were at issue.[36] On any careful analysis, the *Foss* v. *Harbottle* rule is (like any other rule determining *locus standi*) a mixture of substance and procedure.[37]

Further confusion can arise where the court decides to resolve the *Foss* v. *Harbottle* point by referring the matter to the shareholders in general meeting. It may not be clear whether the majority are to resolve whether or not the company should litigate, or whether they are being asked to ratify the wrongdoing that has occurred. In either case the shareholders in a large public company are unlikely to have the information to make a proper judgment of their own interests or those of the company.

---

[31] Sealy, 'The Problems of Standing, Pleading and Proof in Corporate Litigation' in B. G. Pettet (ed.), *Company Law in Change* (Stevens & Sons, 1987), p. 2.

[32] *Ibid.* The issue of enforcing the membership contract is examined below at p. 13.

[33] See further Chapter 2 below.

[34] See, for example, *North West Transportation Co. Ltd* v. *Beatty* (1887) LR 12 App Cas 589 (PC); and *Hogg* v. *Cramphorn Ltd* [1967] Ch 254. See Chapter 2 below.

[35] See *Prudential Assurance Co. Ltd* v. *Newman Industries Ltd (No. 2)* [1982] Ch 204.

[36] See Sealy, 'The Problems of Standing, Pleading and Proof in Corporate Litigation' in B. G. Pettet (ed.), *Company Law in Change* (Stevens & Sons, 1987), p. 3.

[37] See *European Business Law Journal*, May–June 2000, pp. 1–9, in respect of the application of conflicts of laws concepts to the *Foss* v. *Harbottle* rule.

The reform of civil procedure in recent years may enable the courts to provide better answers to some of these problems. In the next chapter, it will be seen that the procedural reform of the derivative action (first introduced in 1994 as Order 15, rule 12A)[38] has brought some clarity, compared with the earlier state of procedural confusion. In one leading case in the Court of Appeal,[39] the process of discovery of documents and the state of the pleadings were described as a 'shambles'. To take one improvement, for example, applications for indemnity orders can now be heard at the stage of the application for leave under rule 12A and its successors.

As the Law Commission's Consultation Paper on shareholder remedies[40] indicates, the courts' case management powers[41] may prove of some assistance in both 'derivative' and 'personal' shareholder suits. However, in Chapter 2 it will be contended that these new case management powers will still not allow the admission of evidence (when the application to bring a derivative suit first comes before the court) about the *prima facie* case against those who have wronged the company. This initial stage will still be confined to arguing the issue of *locus standi* on the basis only of allegations in the pleadings. It will be seen that, in the case of public listed companies, the element of 'wrongdoer control' will still create serious problems for the plaintiff. It would seem that Professor Sealy's proposal for a 'compromise procedure'[42] is not available either in the common law derivative suit[43] or in the Law Commission's proposal for statutory reform.[44]

It is generally considered that the two most significant barriers to successful shareholders' proceedings (especially in the case of derivative suits) are: (a) the difficulty of obtaining, in advance of litigation, adequate evidence to support alleged wrongdoing (even where this is strongly suspected); and (b) the difficulty posed by the great expense of such civil litigation (without any hope of direct personal benefit). In its Report on shareholder remedies,[45] the Law Commission rejected a proposal for 'pre-action discovery' of documents.[46] Similarly, no change

---

[38] See now the Civil Procedure Rules 1998, Schedule 1.

[39] *Prudential Assurance Co. Ltd* v. *Newman Industries Ltd (No. 2)* [1982] Ch 204 at 225.

[40] See Law Commission, *Shareholder Remedies: A Consultation Paper* (Law Commission Consultation Paper No. 142, Stationery Office, 1996), Part 17.

[41] See the Civil Procedure Rules 1998, Part 3.

[42] Sealy, 'The Problems of Standing, Pleading and Proof in Corporate Litigation' in B. G. Pettet (ed.), *Company Law in Change* (Stevens & Sons, 1987), p. 3.

[43] See Chapter 2 below.   [44] See Chapter 3 below.

[45] Law Commission, *Shareholder Remedies* (Law Commission Report No. 246, Cm 3769, Stationery Office, 1997).

[46] See Law Commission, *Shareholder Remedies: A Consultation Paper* (Law Commission Consultation Paper No. 142, Stationery Office, 1996), paras. 7.13–7.16. English law

was made by the Law Commission to existing arrangements for the funding of shareholders' litigation.[47] However, it will be seen that subsequent developments have opened up entirely new possibilities in the guise of 'conditional fee agreements'. It still remains a matter of speculation as to what impact such agreements will have in shareholders' proceedings, whether derivative or personal.[48]

The movement for reform

A dozen years ago, Professor Sealy predicted that, even if Parliament provided a statutory remedy, the 'courts would reinvent just as effective way of saying "go away"'.[49] He later observed that there is an almost palpable judicial resistance in the UK to any move which would allow the individual shareholder any greater access to the courts, and, whatever the legislator may do, this in the long term may continue to be the most potent force against change.[50] This has proved a remarkably accurate prediction. The Law Commission's report on shareholder remedies in 1998, under the chairmanship of a distinguished Chancery judge, retained as much as possible of the rule in *Foss* v. *Harbottle* consistent with creating a statutory derivative action. The other actions by exception to that rule are left unchanged. No change is made to 'substantive' company law and due reverence is paid to the 'proper plaintiff principle' (and other aspects of the *Foss* v. *Harbottle* doctrine) in shaping the structure of the proposed new statutory procedure.[51] Much existing *Foss* v. *Harbottle* jurisprudence finds its niche, in a suitably recast form, in the Law Commission's reformed procedure.[52] It will be seen in Chapter 3[53] that the Law Commission's notion of 'strict judicial control' is considerably more constraining than equivalent Commonwealth legislation.

---

does not confer on shareholders a corporate right to 'internal' company documents. See *Conway* v. *Petronius Clothing Co. Ltd* [1978] 1 WLR 72. The position is different in other common law jurisdictions. See the discussion of section 319 of the Australian Corporations Law by Diana Faber, 'Reform of Shareholders' Remedies' in *Developments in European Company Law* (Kluwer Law, 1998), vol. 1, p. 119 at p. 127.

[47] See Consultation Paper, para. 6.104.   [48] See Chapters 2 and 3 below.

[49] See Sealy, 'The Problems of Standing, Pleading and Proof in Corporate Litigation' in B. G. Pettet (ed.), *Company Law in Change* (Stevens & Sons, 1987), p. 1.

[50] *Ibid.*, p. 16.   [51] See Report, paras. 6.1–6.6. See also paras. 6.80–6.93.

[52] E.g. the role of the independent organ (*ibid.*, para. 6.88), the majority's power to ratify or resolve that no action be taken by the company (*ibid.*, para. 6.87) and the court's power to adjourn proceedings to enable the company to call a meeting (*ibid.*, para. 6.100).

[53] See Chapter 3 at p. 88.

Statutory reform of the *Foss* v. *Harbottle* rule has long been neglected. Although the rule was criticised in both the Cohen[54] and Jenkins[55] reports, no attempt was made to recast or modify it directly. Instead, a statutory procedure to deal with oppression was first introduced in section 210 of the Companies Act 1948 as a result of proposals in the Cohen Report. When this in due time proved inadequate, the Jenkins Report proposed some crucial improvements which eventually produced the modern unfair prejudice remedy.[56] Even this took some eighteen years to be implemented in what was then section 75 of the Companies Act 1980. Although the burgeoning case law on section 459 of the Companies Act 1985, together with developments in the law of just and equitable winding up,[57] catered extremely well for most of the needs of the minority shareholders in private companies, even by the mid-1980s there was perceived to be a need to reform the *Foss* v. *Harbottle* rule in general, and the common law derivative action in particular, by looking to legislative models elsewhere.[58]

There are indications that in 1986 the Department of Trade and Industry were prepared to consider tackling reform of the rule in *Foss* v. *Harbottle* by considering the model provided by the statutory derivative action which spread throughout Canada as part of the federal and provincial legislative reforms of the 1970s. At that time, any proposal of extending a reforming gaze at solutions provided by French and German law were looked at askance. The fact that similar provisions, based in French or German models, were to be found in the draft Fifth Company Law Directive and in the proposed European Company Statute seems to have ruled such an exercise in comparative European law 'off limits'. In the event, no further developments occurred until ten years later, when the Lord Chancellor and the President of DTI requested the Law Commission, *inter alia*, to 'carry out a review of shareholder remedies with particular reference to the rule in *Foss* v. *Harbottle* and its exceptions'.[59]

---

[54] *Report of the Committee on Company Law Amendment* (Cmd 6659, HMSO, London, 1945), paras. 60 and 150.

[55] *Report of the Company Law Committee* (Cmnd 1749, HMSO, London, 1962), paras. 206–8.

[56] See sections 459–461 of the Companies Act 1985. See Chapters 4 and 5 below.

[57] See generally Chapters 4 and 5 below.

[58] See Sealy, 'The Problems of Standing, Pleading and Proof in Corporate Litigation' in B. G. Pettet (ed.), *Company Law in Change* (Stevens & Sons, 1987), p. 16; and Boyle, in B. G. Pettet (ed.), *Company Law in Change* (Stevens & Sons, 1987), pp. 34–5.

[59] The Law Commission's remit also included sections 459–461 of the Companies Act 1985, and the enforcement of shareholder rights under the articles of association. See Consultation Paper, para. 1.2.

In carrying out this task, the Law Commission has likewise avoided any consideration of European company law in any of the Member States of the Union. Perhaps more surprisingly, no serious consideration was given to American corporate law. Commonwealth legislation on the statutory derivative action is of course fully and carefully examined. This may be a pure coincidence, but it is not unreasonable to infer that some degree of guidance as to the scope of the investigation has been given by the DTI. By contrast, in the Law Commission's more recent work on directors' duties, a comparative study of the German law with regard to directors' duties of care and skill[60] was undertaken for the Commission. This did not, of course, involve any examination of the draft Fifth Company Law Directive or the European Company Statute, both of which appear to be regarded as forbidden territory by the DTI.

Minority litigation against listed plcs

It will be seen, when the common law and statutory derivative action are examined in later chapters,[61] that minority shareholders face particular difficulties where they seek redress against a listed public company. Both the defective state of the existing common law, and the detailed design of the new statutory derivative action, cause problems. This state of affairs would seem to reflect an implicit acceptance both by the judiciary and the Law Commission that it is somehow undesirable that large public companies should be exposed to civil litigation by minority shareholders. The enormous size of such bodies and their complex structure, plus their importance in the economy as a whole and to the UK's reputation, make it undesirable, for those who take this view, that a mere minority shareholder should be allowed to cause the havoc that civil litigation may produce. It is assumed that minority shareholders have little directly at stake and that even a successful outcome to the proceedings cannot directly benefit the plaintiffs by doing much to restore the value of their shares. The stock market's lack of confidence may cause a permanent decline in share value, whatever assets are eventually returned to the company. This type of thinking is rarely, if ever, made explicit. However, only such a negative stance[62] can explain the failure to make the derivative action a workable procedure in English law as regards public companies. Civil remedies

---

[60] See Law Commission, *Company Directors: Regulating Conflicts of Interest and Formulating a Statement of Duties. A Joint Consultation Paper* (Law Commission Consultation Paper No. 153, Scottish Law Commission Consultation Paper No. 105, 1998), paras. 12.26–12.37.

[61] See Chapters 2 and 3 below.

[62] See the attitude adopted by the Court of Appeal in *Prudential Assurance Co. Ltd* v. *Newman Industries Ltd (No. 2)* [1982] Ch 204.

(in the form either of a common law shareholder action or as petitioners under section 459) are of course part of the received wisdom in the case of private companies. Here they already flourish and will continue to do so more effectively as a result of the Law Commission's proposals for reform.

It is obviously to be expected that those whose function it is to represent the interests of large public companies (e.g. the CBI and leading firms of City solicitors) will resist any changes in the law which might encourage an 'active' market in civil litigation by minority shareholders. It will be contended that the 'burden' of self-regulation, the investigatory powers of the Department of Trade and Industry, and of course the criminal law, are sufficient to cope with any fraud or mismanagement that may occur in public companies.

Two somewhat contradictory arguments are advanced by those who are hostile to minority litigation involving public companies. First, it is said that the derivative action is largely redundant in such cases and will scarcely even be resorted to in the world of listed plcs. Secondly, it is damaging to the public image of such companies generally, and will rarely produce a beneficial outcome either for the company involved or its shareholders. It would seem unlikely that either of these causes for concern will prove justified simply because the removal of technical barriers preventing derivative litigation against directors and officers of public listed companies becomes a real possibility. There will be cases (as occur in the United States, Canada and Australia) where such proceedings prove amply justified as a mode of redressing serious corporate abuse. Such actions are likely to be relatively uncommon. The vast majority of honestly and competently conducted public companies will continue to thrive with their reputations fully intact.

The contract of association as a source of shareholder remedies

It will be seen that there is some judicial authority that would appear to confer on members a general right to enforce the terms of the articles as a part of the contract of association. On the basis of such judicial *dicta*, taken together with the literal terms of what is now section 14(1) of the Companies Act 1985, some academic writers have asserted that the contract of association may provide a way around the more restrictive aspects of the *Foss* v. *Harbottle* rule. It may also, it is contended, enable shareholders as members to assert what are called 'outsider rights', i.e. rights conferred on members (or indeed non-members) in some other capacity (e.g. as directors or promoters). If this proposition were generally accepted as sound law, it would provide a useful route to bypass the technicalities and obscurities of both the rule and the 'exceptions' to it.

While detailed examination of shareholder actions by exception to the rule (or lying beyond its scope) must be left to Chapter 2, it is appropriate in this chapter to consider the statutory contract of membership as a source of minority shareholders' rights.

The special character of the membership contract

Leaving aside for the moment the issue of 'outsider rights' and the implication of section 14(1) for minority shareholders, it has long been held that the contract of association has a very special character which is impressed upon it by the language of section 14(1). This provides that the memorandum and articles of association when registered bind the company's members to the same extent as if each member had signed and sealed them and they contained a covenant by him or her to observe all provisions contained therein.

The case law on section 14 has long established that it creates an obligation binding alike on members in their dealings with the company,[63] on the company in its dealings with the members as members,[64] and members in their dealings with one another as members.[65] An illustration of an action between members is provided by *Rayfield* v. *Hands*.[66] This case concerned a provision in the articles that imposed a duty on shareholders to purchase the shares of a member who wished to dispose of his holding. It was held that this right could be enforced by virtue of the contract of association. It should be noted that section 14 makes the company a party to the contract of association even though, unlike the members, it is not deemed to have signed and sealed them etc. It is thus not strictly a party to the 'deemed covenant', though bound by the statutory contract. This would seem to result in a different limitation period for claims by the company against its members.[67]

Those seeking to enforce the contract of association are not afforded the same remedies as apply under general contract law (including the law applicable to shareholder agreements). Thus there is no right to damages for breach of the articles (as opposed to liquidated sums due). The contract of association is not defeasible on the grounds of misrepresentation, mistake in law or equity, undue influence or duress.[68] Thus the

---

[63] *Bradford Banking Co.* v. *Henry Briggs & Co.* (1886) 12 App Cas 29 (HL); *Wood* v. *Odessa Waterworks Co.* (1889) 42 ChD 636; and *Quin & Axtens* v. *Salmon* [1909] AC 442 (HL).

[64] *Oak Bank Oil Co.* v. *Crum* (1882) 8 App Cas 65 at 116.

[65] *Eley* v. *Positive Government Security Life Assurance Co.* (1876) 1 Ex D 88 (CA).

[66] [1960] Ch 1.

[67] See Law Commission, *Shareholder Remedies* (Law Commission Report No. 246, Cm 3769, Stationery Office, 1997), para. 7.3. See *ibid.* as to the historical origins of the statutory formula now embodied in section 14(1).

[68] *Bratton Seymour Service Co. Ltd* v. *Oxborough* [1992] BCLC 693 at 695 (CA).

articles cannot be rectified on the ground of mistake.[69] In *Bratton Seymour Services Ltd* v. *Oxborough*,[70] the Court of Appeal refused to imply a term into the articles on the basis of business efficacy which would have the effect of imposing on a member an obligation to make a financial contribution to certain expenses incurred by the company. The court indicated that terms would not readily be implied into the articles from extrinsic circumstances.[71] This was because of the special nature of the contract with its impact on future shareholders[72] (and other third parties) who had a right to rely on the articles as registered unless they have been validly altered by special resolution.

'Outsider rights' in the articles

In accordance with normal contractual principles, those who are not members cannot enforce the provisions of the articles either against the company or its members.[73] A special feature of the section 14 contract is that even a member cannot enforce provisions for his benefit in some capacity other than that of member: e.g. he cannot assert a right to be appointed solicitor, secretary or director[74] by reason of provisions contained only in the articles. So an article providing for the reference of disputes to arbitration may be enforceable by or against a member in his capacity as such, but not in some other capacity, e.g. that of director.[75] On the other hand, the shareholder is not bound in his personal capacity: 'The purpose of the memorandum and articles is to define the position of the shareholder as shareholder, not to bind him in his capacity as an individual.'[76]

This special feature has received substantial criticism from some academic commentators. It is objected that it rests solely upon Astbury J's

---

[69] *Scott* v. *Frank F Scott (London) Ltd* [1990] Ch 796.
[70] [1992] BCLC 693 at 696 *per* Dillon LJ and at 698 *per* Steyn LJ.
[71] See *Mutual Life Insurance Co.* v. *Rank Organisation* [1985] BCLC 11.
[72] I.e. under section 9 of the Companies Act 1985.
[73] *Re Rotherham Chemical Co.* (1883) 25 ChD 103; *Melhado* v. *Porto Allegre Co.* (1874) LR 9 CP 503; *Re Empress Engineering Co.* (1881) 16 ChD 125 (CA); and *Re English and Colonial Produce Co.* [1906] 2 Ch 435.
[74] *Eley* v. *Positive Government Security Life Assurance Co.* (1876) 1 Ex D 88 (CA); and *Browne* v. *La Trinidad* (1888) 37 ChD 1. See, however, the Contracts (Rights of Third Parties) Act 1999.
[75] *Hickman* v. *Kent or Romney Marsh Sheep-Breeders' Association* [1915] 1 Ch 881; *Beattie* v. *E and F Beattie* [1938] Ch 708; and *London Sack and Bag Co.* v. *Dixon* [1943] 2 All ER 763 (CA).
[76] *Bisgood* v. *Henderson's Transvaal Estates* [1908] 1 Ch 743 at 759 (CA) *per* Buckley LJ. See also *Baring-Gould* v. *Sharpington Combined Pick and Shovel Syndicate* [1899] 2 Ch 80 (CA).

decision in *Hickman* v. *Kent or Romney Marsh Sheep-Breeders' Association*.[77] It is argued that his decision conflicts with earlier decisions which do not recognise the principle which Astbury J attempted to elicit from them. Moreover, it is said that the *Hickman* principle appears to ignore the wording of what is now section 14(1) of the Companies Act 1985, which creates a contractual obligation in respect of 'all the provisions of the memorandum and of the articles'. The view contended for by these commentators is that an 'outsider', so long as he sues in his capacity as shareholder, can compel the company not to depart from the contract with him under the articles. This is so even if that results indirectly in the enforcement of 'outsider' rights vested in third parties or in the plaintiff shareholder.

The somewhat unclear wording of section 14 (and its predecessors, e.g. section 16 of the 1862 Act and section 20 of the 1948 Act) long gave rise to conflicting judicial interpretation. This stemmed in part from the fact that, though the memorandum and articles 'shall, when registered, bind the company and the members', this is based on a putative statutory signing and sealing by the members and not by the company.[78] Likewise, the memorandum and articles are deemed to contain 'covenants on the part of each member' (but not the company) to observe their provisions.[79] Until the end of the nineteenth century the courts were divided as to the parties to this statutory contract of association (i.e. parties in the sense of having rights of action and liabilities thereunder). There were authorities both for and against there being a contract between the members *inter se*,[80] as well as both for and against section 14 creating a contract between the company and its members.[81]

As indicated above, the modern law was eventually settled that the section 14 contract confers rights between the company and its members and between the members *inter se*. However, the still conflicting reasoning

---

[77] [1915] 1 Ch 881. See Gregory, 'The Section 20 Contract' (1981) 44 *Modern Law Review* 526. This amplifies the views earlier expressed by Lord Wedderburn, (1957) *Cambridge Law Journal* 194 at 212–13. See further Wedderburn, (1989) 52 *Modern Law Review* 401. This is a case note on *Breckland Group Holdings* v. *London & Suffolk Properties Ltd* [1989] BCLC 100.

[78] See above.

[79] The explanation of this omission lies in the conveyancing background to this section. See Gregory, 'The Section 20 Contract' (1981) 44 *Modern Law Review* 526 at 528–9. Under the Joint Stock Companies Act 1844, each shareholder executed an indenture with a trustee for the company. This incorporated or referred to the company's constitution. This requirement was dropped in the Joint Stock Companies Act 1856. The covenant was simply deemed to exist by the statute but no covenant with the company was expressed.

[80] Compare *Eley* v. *Positive Government Security Life Assurance Co.* (1876) 1 Ex D 88 at 89 (CA), with *Welton* v. *Saffrey* [1897] AC 299 at 315 *per* Lord Herschell.

[81] Compare *Johnson* v. *Lyttle's Iron Agency* (1877) 5 ChD 687 at 993 with *Browne* v. *La Trinidad* (1888) 37 ChD 1 at 12 and 15.

in the cases (considered by Astbury J in *Hickman*) induced his attempt to provide a perhaps novel reconciling principle with regard to the scope of the contractual effect of the articles.[82] It must be readily conceded that the case law is still in a state of some confusion, and that in some situations the courts have allowed a member, suing as such, to enforce a non-shareholder right conferred by the articles. This has been done to protect shareholder-directors whose rights to hold office, or to participate in management, or to exercise a veto over board decisions, or to commence litigation, have been brushed aside in breach of a provision in the articles.[83] However, it is a long step from this to conclude that every shareholder has a right to have all and every one of the articles enforced by declaration or injunction.[84] To do so is to ignore not only the authorities on the *Hickman* principle which, whatever its questionable provenance, has never been overruled and has been applied by the Court of Appeal.[85] It also overlooks the rule in *Foss* v. *Harbottle* and the related question of the majority shareholders' right to ratify some, but not all, breaches of the articles.[86] The Court of Appeal has, on more than one occasion, indicated that the members' contract of association cannot be used to 'short-circuit' the rule in *Foss* v. *Harbottle*, especially in the case of shareholders' actions to remedy directors' breaches of fiduciary duty to the company.[87] This is clearly of more significance than the confusion of the courts in the late nineteenth century as to the parties to the statutory contract of association.[88]

---

[82] The earlier cases were influenced by grounds other than the *Hickman* principle: e.g. the old view that members were not parties to the contract (*Baring-Gould* v. *Sharpington Combined Pick and Shovel Syndicate* [1899] 2 Ch 80), or that the article in question was directory rather than mandatory (*Pritchard's Case* (1873) 8 Ch App 956 at 960), or that the plaintiff, as a matter of procedural form, sued not as a member but in some external capacity (e.g. as a solicitor or promoter) (*Eley* v. *Positive Government Security Life Assurance Co.* (1876) 1 Ex D 88 (CA)). See (1981) 44 *Modern Law Review* 526 at 531–9.

[83] E.g. *Imperial Hydropathic Hotel* v. *Hamson* (1882) 23 ChD 1; *Pulbrook* v. *Richmond Consolidated Mining Co.* (1878) 9 ChD 610; *Quin & Axtens* v. *Salmon* [1909] AC 442; *Hayes* v. *Bristol Plant Hire* [1957] 1 All ER 688; and *Breckland Group Holdings Ltd* v. *London and Suffolk Properties Ltd* [1989] BCLC 100, noted by Wedderburn, (1989) 52 *Modern Law Review* 401. Attempts have been made by commentators to explain, on 'organic' or constitutional grounds, when the courts will allow 'non-shareholder rights' in the articles to be enforced. See Goldberg, (1972) 35 *Modern Law Review* 362; Bastin (1977) J BL 17; and Prentice, (1980) 1 *Company Lawyer* 179.

[84] It is clear that (claims for arrears of dividend and the like aside) damages will not be awarded for breach of this very special contract. This alone may indicate its special character: a case perhaps of *ibi remedium, ubi jus*.

[85] *Beattie* v. *E and F Beattie Ltd* [1938] Ch 708 at 713–14. See also *London Sack and Bag Co. Ltd* v. *Dixon* [1943] 2 All ER 763.

[86] See *Grant* v. *UK Switchback Railways* (1889) 40 ChD 135 (CA).

[87] See *Bamford* v. *Bamford* [1970] Ch 212; and *Prudential Assurance Co. Ltd* v. *Newman Industries Ltd (No. 2)* [1982] Ch 204. See the further discussion of these issues in Chapter 2, p. 28 below.

[88] See further R. R. Drury, 'The Relative Nature of a Shareholders' Right to Enforce the Company Contract' (1986) *Cambridge Law Journal* 219. This is an interesting attempt

Steyn LJ's observations in *Bratton Seymour Service Co. Ltd* v. *Oxborough*[89] would appear to conclude the debate on 'outsiders rights' as far as the courts are concerned:

> It is, however, a statutory contract of a special nature with its own distinctive features. It derives its binding force not from a bargain struck between the parties but from the terms of the statute. It is binding only in so far as it affects the rights and obligations between the company and the members acting in their capacity as members. If it contains provisions conferring rights and obligations on outsiders, then these provisions do not bite as part of the contract between the company and the members, even if the outsider is co-incidentally a member.

Although Steyn LJ does not refer to the *Foss* v. *Harbottle* rule, his observations are entirely consistent with that rule. Mere breaches of the articles which do not amount to an infringement of an individual membership right (such as the right to vote) are ratifiable and are therefore not actionable by a minority shareholder. Likewise there can be no contractual right for shareholders to enforce directors' duties as an incident of the contract of membership.[90]

In reviewing the existing law in its Consultation Paper on shareholder remedies, the Law Commission takes the same view that case law does not support a generalised right of action based on the section 14 membership contract.[91] It then considers the possibility of reforming section 14 'by clarification of the types of situation that may fall within the section'.[92] The Commission toyed with the suggestion that a reformed section 14 should include a list of personal shareholder rights enforceable under the section. 'The reformed section might provide a non-exhaustive list of rights which the courts have to date allowed shareholders to enforce by personal action under the section. The statute could indicate that the fact that these rights can be enforced by personal action does not mean that there are no others that can be enforced by the same means.' Scope is thus left for judicial initiative.

In the event, the Consultation Paper 'provisionally recommended against this idea'. The Law Commission points to the problem that not every breach of the articles could be made actionable and the difficulty of

---

to reconcile the cases on the basis that the courts weigh various factors in the balance in deciding whether to enforce the shareholders' 'relative right'. See further at p. 20 below.

[89] [1992] BCLC 693 at 698.

[90] See *Prudential Assurance Co. Ltd* v. *Newman Industries Ltd (No. 2)* [1982] Ch 204 at 210–21. Compare *Bamford* v. *Bamford* [1968] 3 WLR 317 (Plowman J at first instance). See Wedderburn, (1968) 31 *Modern Law Review* 688 at 691–2.

[91] Consultation Paper, paras. 2.6–2.28.   [92] *Ibid.*, paras. 20.2–20.4.

deciding where to draw the line. In its Report on shareholder remedies,[93] the Law Commission reaches the same conclusion with the support of its consultees. This is clearly consistent with a policy against undertaking the difficult and delicate task of attempting to reform the rule in *Foss* v. *Harbottle* as a whole. The Law Commission decided at an early stage that only the derivative action was appropriate grist for its reforming mill. This limitation was self-imposed since the terms of its remit from the Lord Chancellor and the President of the Board of Trade were expressed in wider terms so as to include 'the rule in *Foss* v. *Harbottle* and its exceptions'.[94] This policy decision leaves the mysteries and obscurities that surround both the membership contract, and the precise scope of the personal actions available to shareholders, in their existing state of untidy confusion.[95]

A recent consultation paper from the Company Law Review Steering Group[96] suggests reversing the Law Commission's approach to shareholders' individual rights under the company's constitution. Instead of leaving shareholders' individual rights unreformed, together with the uncertain implications of the section 14 contract of association, a more radical solution is proposed. The company's constitution will have a purely statutory status rather than the putatively contractual basis, as now. Shareholders' individual rights will take the form of 'personal rights under the constitution'.[97] The proposed legislation will expressly set out the extent to which it gives rise to obligations binding on the company and enforceable by the company's members. These personal rights will be unaffected by ratification. The legislation would also provide for remedies (including damages) available for enforcement of these rights. Such rights would be enforceable by the company and by members in their capacity as members as such and as outsiders. Outsiders (including directors) would not have rights under the constitution.

The further implications of these proposals, which are still subject to consultation, will be explored in the next chapter.[98] If implemented, these proposals would appear to put the whole question of minority shareholders' actions on a statutory footing. The *Foss* v. *Harbottle* rule in its traditional form would disappear.

---

[93] Law Commission, *Shareholder Remedies* (Law Commission Report No. 246, Cm 3769, Stationery Office, 1997), paras. 7.2–7.11.

[94] *Ibid.*, para. 1.1. See likewise the Consultation Paper, para. 1.2.

[95] See further Chapter 2 below.

[96] See DTI Company Law Review Steering Group, *Modern Company Law for a Competitive Economy: Developing the Framework* (DTI, URN 00/656, March 2000), paras. 4.87–4.99.

[97] See *ibid.*, para. 4.99.   [98] See Chapter 2, p. 55 below.

Theorising *Foss* v. *Harbottle*

Robert Drury's well-known article on the members' contract[99] embodies a rare attempt to provide a theoretical underpinning to the rule in *Foss* v. *Harbottle*. It is constructed upon two interrelated bases. The first is an attempt to reconcile the case law on the membership contract (including the problem of outsider rights) with the body of case law on the *Foss* v. *Harbottle* rule. The second is to draw upon the research work undertaken in America[100] and the UK[101] on relational contracts. This has demonstrated the significance of the distinction between two types of commercial contract – the short-term contract of economic exchange (e.g. in goods or services) as opposed to the long-term 'relational contract'. Where the parties are in such a long-term contract (or series of renewable contracts) the evidence from this research is that both parties try to find other means than litigation to resolve any disputes about performance that may arise. This may involve 'contractual planning' (e.g. provision of arbitration or liquidated damages clauses) or may employ non-contractual solutions such as withholding performance or payment. The ongoing relationship is regarded as more important than resorting to litigation which is all too likely finally to disrupt the relationship.

Drury transposes this experience to the corporate setting. He argues that the relationship between the company and its shareholders may be characterised as just such a long-term contractual relationship. The *Foss* v. *Harbottle* rule can thus be given a theoretical framework. The courts have sought, it is contended, to provide a balance between the rights of individual shareholders under the terms of the company's constitution and the rights of other shareholders (especially those constituting a majority) who may well have conflicting rights. This, of course, includes the right of a three-quarters majority to alter the constitution. The jurisdiction of the majority within the 'internal forum' of the company must, as the courts have long held, be respected. The company's internal dispute-resolution machinery must be supported. Thus litigation should only be permitted where it involves matters which cannot in law be ratified by a general meeting of shareholders or where the majority have indicated they support the minority's grievances.

In broad outline this furnishes a persuasive theoretical framework to illuminate the purposes and policy behind the rule. Clearly, an unrestricted

---

[99] R. R. Drury, 'The Relative Nature of a Shareholders' Right to Enforce the Company Contract' (1986) *Cambridge Law Journal* 219.

[100] S. Macaulay, 'Non-Contractual Relations in Business: A Preliminary Study' (1963) 28 *American Sociological Review* 55.

[101] Beale and Dugdale, 'Contracts Between Businessmen: Planning and the Use of Contractual Remedies' (1975) 2 *British Journal of Law and Society* 45.

right to litigate for every breach of the articles, or other procedural irregularities in the conduct of meetings, would disrupt the orderly conduct of the company's affairs. It would undermine the long-term relationships between shareholders because of what Drury and others describe as the 'polarising effect' of litigation. Thus in general where corporate litigation is contemplated there must be majority support, or at any rate the endorsement of the board of directors acting in the name of the company as a whole.

Difficulties with this theory

The main difficulty with this theory is that it imbues the detailed case law under the *Foss* v. *Harbottle* rubric with a coherence and rationality which in many respects it lacks. Professor Sealy,[102] as has already been noted, has amply demonstrated that many individual cases applying the rule have an 'off-hand' character which cannot be reconciled with genuine corporate principles based on carefully thought out policies. In the next chapter, the shortcomings in the existing law will be examined in detail. Here it is sufficient to summarise the main areas where difficulties appear to exist, or the law lacks precision and clarity:

1. The duty of a majority of shareholders to act *bona fide* in the interests of the company in exercising the statutory power to alter the articles of association.
2. The concept of 'class rights' and what counts as an 'infringement' of class rights (such rights attract additional statutory protection).
3. Where the line is to be drawn between shareholders' individual rights and mere internal irregularities.
4. The distinction between a 'mere breach' of the articles and an informal departure from their terms.

Implicit in the last two headings, as well as the cause of other difficulties, is the whole question of the power of the majority to ratify wrongful or irregular conduct. Thus it is not always clear precisely where the line is drawn between what is 'ratifiable' as opposed to 'non-ratifiable'. Even where this line is clear, the policy behind the distinction may be dubious. Why is it that a breach of a director's duty of care and skill is ratifiable? Corporate law scholars, it will be seen, continue to argue about the line to be drawn between the 'no conflict' cases and those where equitable fraud (or breach of trust) is found. The most debatable issue of all is

---

[102] See pp. 7–8 above.

that it is 'ratifiability' not actual ratification by the majority that will bar a minority action.

This latter point hardly squares with the theory of 'relative rights' of minority shareholders. These rights, it is contended,[103] are subject to the rights of every other shareholder to condone or ratify breaches of internal managerial procedures: 'adjudication between these conflicting rights is then best accomplished by reference to the machinery provided by company law, namely, by taking into account the wishes of the majority to see which they support. Such an approach would facilitate (but not guarantee) the resolution of the dispute without recourse to harmful litigation.'

Even where a shareholders' meeting is seized of the matter, its prophylactic function is open to serious question. Few company meetings are conducted in the form of a meeting of a nineteenth-century benevolent association or a New England town meeting. In reality, company meetings are as widely varied as companies themselves. The meetings of listed public companies are vastly different in their social reality and psychodynamics from those of even the most substantial private companies. In the case of small corporate partnerships, meetings may be entirely dispensed with and replaced with a 'written resolution' procedure. In truth, the judicially created norms, stemming from 'majority rule' and the power to ratify, are heavily imbued with legal formalism. They exist to enable the court to open or close the gate to minority shareholders. The real equivalents to 'contractual planning' in true 'relational contracts' are to be found in provisions in the articles adopted by those who have formed the company or at a later stage. Obvious examples are 'pre-emption rights' in the articles allowing minority shareholders to require that their shares be bought by the majority. Likewise there is the provision in the articles for arbitration of disputes and for the company's auditor to value the shares of dissenting shareholders.[104]

The use of statutory remedies to 'bypass' the *Foss* v. *Harbottle* rule

Since the Companies Act 1948, there has been a statutory remedy to enable minority shareholders to seek relief by petition to the court. Since the Companies Act 1980 recast this remedy on the basis of 'unfair prejudice', the courts have greatly expanded the availability of this form of redress.[105] It is a commonplace observation of company law textbooks that minority

---

[103] See R. R. Drury, 'The Relative Nature of a Shareholders' Right to Enforce the Company Contract' (1986) *Cambridge Law Journal* 219 at 238–9.
[104] See Consultation Paper, paras. 19.12–19.16.   [105] See Chapters 4 and 5 below.

shareholders tend today to seek relief by means of a section 459 petition for unfair prejudice rather than by common law actions under the 'exceptions' to *Foss* v. *Harbottle*. This is particularly the case where the nature of a minority shareholder's grievance does not fall squarely within one of the established grounds for giving relief under those exceptions.[106]

The use of derivative actions to redress wrongs to the company has already been shown to cause particular problems. To a limited extent, the remedies provided under section 461 (notably the power to litigate on behalf of the company) may provide a substitute for a derivative action at common law.[107] (This, of course, assumes that the petition has already persuaded the court that the 'unfair prejudice' test in section 459 has been met.) It remains true, however, that the unfair prejudice remedy is overwhelmingly used to remedy the personal grievances of minority shareholders, and the form of relief sought under section 461 is a 'buyout' of the minority's shares by the majority. In Chapter 3, it will be seen that the Law Commission, in its report on shareholder remedies, has recognised the severe limitation both of the common law derivative action and of the section 459 procedure as a possible substitute. The Commission seeks to meet the need for an effective replacement of the common law derivative action by a new statutory derivative action based on Commonwealth legal models.

None of this speaks well of the existing law on shareholders' actions at common law. It is perhaps not too much to say that the common law procedures may well be left to wither on the vine while the statutory remedies flourish. Certainly, the obscurity and complexity of the *Foss* v. *Harbottle* rule cannot be described as a model of judicial policy-making.

---

[106] See the problem areas listed above and the discussion of shareholders' action by exception to the rule in Chapter 2 below.

[107] See Chapter 5 below.

2 Shareholder actions by exception to the rule

Direct and derivative actions

The type of shareholders' remedy first explored in this chapter is the derivative action. This will be examined both in respect of the substantive law grounds on which such an action may be based and, later, of its procedural character. The scope of the common law derivative action[1] is defined by the nature of the remedy which is sought. A derivative action is concerned with recovering damages, property or funds which belong to the company for wrongs done to it. In most cases, this involves a serious breach of directors' duties, but the derivative form of action is only appropriate where recovery for the company will result from a successful judgment. Where the remedy sought is an injunction or declaration to prevent an abuse of power by directors, the action is not properly classified as derivative. This distinction has been amply clarified in the case of actions based on *ultra vires* activities. Where the plaintiff shareholder seeks only to restrain a proposed *ultra vires* transaction, the action will not take the derivative form. In contrast, where the plaintiff seeks to 'unscramble' an existing *ultra vires* transaction, the recovery of property (and possibly damage for breach of duty by directors) necessitates that the proceeding takes the derivative form.[2]

Extensive attention is given in this chapter to the problems posed by the derivative action. The Court of Appeal's decision in *Prudential Assurance Co. Ltd* v. *Newman Industries Ltd (No. 2)*[3] was widely viewed as heralding the 'death knell' of the derivative action so far as public companies were concerned. It will be contended, however, that when more recent procedural reforms are taken into account this dismissive view of the derivative action is far from being justified. It is still quite regularly employed in the case of private companies.

---

[1] As to the scope of the proposed statutory derivative action, see Chapter 3, p. 62 below.
[2] See *Russell* v. *Wakefield Waterworks* (1875) LR 20 Eq 474; and *Taylor* v. *NUM* [1985] BCLC 237. Under the current DTI programme of reform, what remains of *ultra vires* will disappear. These cases still illustrate the procedural distinction.
[3] [1987] Ch 204.

An extended overview of the American derivative action is given to put the English procedure in a comparative context.[4] The abuse of the American derivative action by means of 'strike suits' is sometimes pointed out as a warning against any relaxation in the English concept of 'fraud on a minority' in providing a 'narrow gateway' to such actions here.[5] It will, however, be seen that the more restrictive approach in contemporary American law is still more amenable to derivative suits than is English law. Some attention will be given to the French and German law approach to derivative action. This is based on a threshold percentage shareholding by the minority. In the case of public listed companies, this still imposes a significant hurdle. It has certainly not encouraged abusive litigation by minority shareholders.

The last part of this chapter deals with what may best be collectively described as 'direct' shareholder actions. Essentially, the plaintiff minority shareholder, or a group of such, seeks personal redress against the company for what amounts to a breach of the constitution or an infringement of shareholders' individual rights (or class rights).[6] The common justification for such proceedings as being 'beyond' the *Foss* v. *Harbottle* rule is that the misconduct alleged is not capable of ratification by a simple majority of shareholders. It will be seen that such actions may, in the appropriate circumstances, be brought either in the form of an individual shareholder action or in the representative form on behalf of other shareholders similarly affected.

The derivative action

The fraud on a minority 'exception'

The two linked elements in the concept of fraud on a minority were established in a leading Privy Council decision at the beginning of the last century.[7] In a passage in his judgment, which has been frequently quoted and was later adopted by the Privy Council in another case,[8] Lord Davey maintains that an exception would be made to the principle that the company is a proper plaintiff where 'the persons against whom relief is sought themselves hold and control the majority of shares in the

---

[4] The Commonwealth legislative developments are considered in Chapter 3 below.

[5] This concern may even have influenced the Law Commission in framing its proposals for a new statutory derivative action. See Chapter 3 below.

[6] The minority shareholders' right to petition for 'unfair prejudice' is dealt with separately in Chapters 4 and 5 below.

[7] See *Burland* v. *Earle* [1902] AC 83 at 93.

[8] *Dominion Cotton Mills* v. *Amyot* [1912] AC 546 (PC); see also *Cook* v. *Deeks* [1916] 1 AC 554 (PC); and *Foster* v. *Foster* [1918] 1 Ch 532 at 547.

company and will not permit an action to be brought in the name of the company'. This has come to be known as the element of 'wrongdoer control' and will be examined further below.[9]

Fraudulent character of alleged breaches

The second element concerns the kind of wrongful conduct by directors for which the minority may maintain a derivative action. Such actions are confined to situations 'in which the acts complained of are of a fraudulent character or are beyond the powers of the company. A familiar example is where the majority are endeavouring directly or indirectly to appropriate to themselves money or property, or advantages which belong to the company, or in which the other shareholders are entitled to participate.'[10] Later cases established that misappropriation of corporate property extends to property (or contracts) which 'belong in equity' to the company.[11] In such cases, the directors are accountable for a non-ratifiable breach of trust and not merely for a breach of their fiduciary duties.

Some academic commentators have found difficulty in distinguishing between 'breach of trust' or a 'misappropriation of corporate assets' and a mere breach of fiduciary duties where this involves an infringement merely of the 'no-conflict rule'.[12] Such commentators find difficulty in distinguishing between the reasoning in the classic 'secret profits' House of Lords decision in *Regal (Hastings) v. Gulliver*[13] and that of the Privy Council in *Cook v. Deeks.*[14] Nevertheless, as these commentators admit, this distinction has to be accepted as critical to the issue of which types of breach of duty amount to 'equitable fraud' and are therefore incapable of ratification. The distinction between 'ratifiable' and 'non-ratifiable' breaches of directors' duties has, of course, significance not only for minority shareholder actions but also for corporate actions (i.e. brought by the company itself).[15]

Essentially, the courts, as a matter of conscience and public policy, have had to 'ring fence' directorial misbehaviour which goes beyond certain ethical limits. The shareholders' power to ratify 'mere' breaches of fiduciary duty (including the duty of care and skill) has never been allowed

---

[9] See p. 27 below.   [10] [1912] AC 83 at 93.
[11] *Cook v. Deeks* [1916] 1 AC 554 (PC).
[12] See P. L. Davies (ed.), *Gower's Principles of Modern Company Law* (6th ed., London, Sweet & Maxwell, 1997), p. 467, and *Farrar's Company Law* (3rd ed., Butterworths, 1991), p. 421.
[13] [1967] 2 AC 134n, [1942] 1 All ER 378 (HL).   [14] [1916] AC 554 (PC).
[15] See *Industrial Development Consultants v. Cooley* [1972] 1 WLR 443; and *Island Export Finance Ltd v. Umunna* [1986] BCLC 46.

to extend further than incidental secret profit so as to absolve gains made at the expense of the company.[16] In *Daniels* v. *Daniels*,[17] Templeman J, in reviewing the earlier authorities, stated the principle which he 'gleaned' from the earlier case law: a minority shareholder who has no other remedy may sue where directors use their powers, intentionally or unintentionally, fraudulently or negligently, in a manner which benefits themselves at the expense of the company.[18]

Wrongdoer control

The key question about the need to establish 'wrongdoer control' is how this element of 'fraud on a minority' as a ground for a derivative action can be established to the court's satisfaction in the case of public listed companies. In such companies, widely dispersed shareholdings make strict *de jure* control of a majority of shares by the wrongdoing directors and their associates very unlikely. In such a situation, the strict test of *de jure* control demanded in *Pavlides* v. *Jensen*[19] can hardly ever be met. This requires the wrongdoers to own (directly or by nominees) at least 51 per cent of the voting shares. Earlier cases took a more realistic and less demanding approach to wrongdoer control. This was linked with more flexible formulation if the exceptions to shareholders' action by exception to the *Foss* v. *Harbottle* rule. This was originally encapsulated by Jessel MR in *Russell* v. *Wakefield Waterworks*[20] in the observation that the *Foss* v. *Harbottle* rule 'is not a universal rule; that is, it is a rule subject to exceptions, and the exceptions depend very much on the necessity of the case; that is the necessity of the court doing justice'.

In his first instance judgment in *Prudential Assurance Co. Ltd* v. *Newman Industries Ltd (No. 2)*,[21] Vinelott J developed this flexible approach to *de facto* control by the alleged wrongdoing directors. The court found that there was no real possibility that the question whether the company should commence proceedings would ever be put to the shareholders in a way that would enable them to exercise a proper judgment as to whether it was in the company's interest that litigation should be commenced. Unless the minority could be allowed to sue on the company's behalf, the interests of justice would be defeated, in that an action which ought to be pursued on behalf of the company could not be pursued. On this view, 'wrongdoer

---

[16] See further Boyle, 'Attorney-General v. Reid: The Company Law Implications' (1995) 16 *Company Lawyer* 131–2.
[17] [1978] Ch 406.   [18] *Ibid.* at 414.   [19] [1956] Ch 565.
[20] (1875) LR 20 Eq 474 at 480. Applied in *Heyting* v. *Dupont* [1964] 2 WLR 843 (CA). See also *Hodgson* v. *NALGO* [1972] 1 WLR 130 at 140. This 'fifth exception' or 'fall back' position is discussed at p. 31 below.
[21] [1980] 2 All ER 841 at 871–7.

control' comprehends *de facto* control of the company (as well as *de jure* control of the kind required in *Pavlides* v. *Jensen*).[22]

Perhaps unfortunately, the Court of Appeal[23] would have none of this. First of all, the Court (on appeal from Vinelott J) repudiated the whole 'justice of the case' principle as a ground for departing from the rule in *Foss* v. *Harbottle*, and therefore as the theoretical basis employed by Vinelott J. The court was fully aware of the procedural difficulties caused by *de facto* control of public companies,[24] but remained unconvinced that Vinelott J's test of '*de facto* control' was a practical test, particularly as it involved a full dress trial before that test is applied.

Instead, the Court of Appeal suggested that 'it may well be right' for a judge trying the preliminary issue to grant a sufficient adjournment to enable a meeting of shareholders to be convened by the board. This enables the judge to reach a conclusion (as to wrongdoer control) in the light of the conduct of and proceedings at the meeting. Where the company has an independent board possessed of adequate information, then the board is entitled to make a commercial assessment of the advantage to the company in taking civil proceedings (whether that assessment be sound or unsound). Where a shareholders' meeting is summoned, it seems that its function is not to ratify or approve an exercise of power by a director. Instead, the meeting's function, in the event they do not adopt the proceedings initiated by the minority, is to help clarify the judge's mind as to whether or not wrongdoer control exists. This ignores the difficulty of determining the motivation and conflicting interests of various shareholders at a company meeting. For example, in the *Prudential* case itself, both an 'independent' board and a 'controlled' meeting of shareholders were successfully misled by the defendants.

In a case involving a substantial private company, *Smith* v. *Croft (No. 2)*,[25] Knox J introduced an innovative method of determining whether wrongdoer control existed. If the defendant was able to point to an 'appropriate independent organ' of the company that had decided that it was not in the commercial interest of the company to pursue the action, it could not proceed. In *Smith* v. *Croft*, a majority of shareholders within the minority was allowed to decide. The court held that such an independent majority within the minority must reach its conclusions on grounds genuinely thought to advance the company's interests. Its decision is then treated as that of a 'corporate independent organ' which

---

[22] [1956] Ch 565.   [23] [1982] Ch 204.

[24] The Court of Appeal observed that the term 'control' embraces a broad spectrum extending from an overall majority of votes at one end, to a majority of votes at the other end made up of those likely to be cast by the delinquent himself, plus those voting with him as a result of influence and apathy.

[25] [1988] Ch 114.

can properly prevent the plaintiff shareholders from suing. It is for the judge to determine whether the 'majority within the minority' has fairly reached its decision. It is not his function to say whether its decision is right or wrong.

This approach to the issue of wrongdoer control may make derivative actions extremely difficult to bring except in the smallest private companies.[26]

The aftermath of the Prudential case

In spite of the despondent tone of most of the scholarly comments[27] published in the immediate aftermath of the *Prudential* case,[28] and the apparent reinforcement of this by Knox J's decision in *Smith* v. *Croft*,[29] with the passage of time it has perhaps become clear to those same commentators that the Court of Appeal's decision need not cast such a gloomy light on the prospects of derivative litigation even in the case of listed plcs – where *de facto* control by the wrongdoers creates problems. Professor Gower's 'calamity' may not in the long run prove to be the disaster he portended.

It is readily apparent, even from the headnote to the *Prudential* case, that the Court of Appeal's observations were (and are) wholly *obiter*. They should perhaps be taken as no more than 'notes for guidance' for future courts as to how and at what stage 'wrongdoer control' and other aspects of 'fraud on a minority' should be dealt with by the court. The actual history of the litigation in the *Prudential* case amply demonstrates how inadequate the solutions outlined by the Court of Appeal were. Before the full hearing at first instance, the general meeting were clearly misled as to the true situation, and the independent majority of the board of directors 'changed sides' before the matter came before the Court of Appeal. They were obviously convinced by what the trial and Vinelott J's judgment had told them about the true interests of their company. Had the trial judge himself followed the Court of Appeal's guidelines, the *Prudential* case would not have gone to trial at all. Only a 'thirty-day action' awoke the independent majority on the board. As others have pointed out, the Court of Appeal's policy guidelines do not accord with some earlier decisions either (i) as to the preliminary stage at which the *Foss* v. *Harbottle* point

---

[26] Where the shareholders are divided into two 'camps', the 'independent organ' will not be discoverable. In *Barrett* v. *Duckett* [1995] 1 BCLC 73, it was held that a 50 per cent shareholder may count as a minority shareholder in a derivative action. The finding on wrongdoer control was upheld in the Court of Appeal: [1995] 1 BCLC 243. See also *Welsh* v. *Nilsson* [1961] NZLR 64 (CA of New Zealand).

[27] See L. C. B. Gower, *Gower's Principles of Modern Company Law* (5th ed., London, Sweet & Maxwell, 1992), pp. 647–62; and P. L. Davies (ed.), *Gower's Principles of Modern Company Law* (6th ed., London, Sweet & Maxwell, 1997), pp. 673–6.

[28] [1982] Ch 204 (CA).   [29] [1988] Ch 114.

must be taken[30] or (ii) as to how the question of wrongdoer control in public companies should be resolved.[31] Surely it must still be open not only to the House of Lords but also to a future Court of Appeal to review and restate (or indeed overturn) the guidelines given by the Court of Appeal in *Prudential* and to do so in a more flexible and liberal spirit. There would seem to be no reason why the approach taken by the Australian court in *Hurley* v. *BGH Nominees* should not be adopted here. It may be useful to quote a passage from Chief Justice King's judgment in the Supreme Court of South Australia:[32]

I do not think that the procedure suggested in *Prudential* v. *Newman* could be applied in all cases. In many cases a hearing to determine whether there was a *prima facie* case would be almost as long as a full trial and a good deal less satisfactory. In such cases, the only reasonable course may be to determine the issue of standing, if raised as a preliminary issue, on the assumption that the allegations in the statement of claim are correct. Even on that basis it may be desirable to distinguish sharply between the issue whether allegations in the statement of claim, if true, disclose the legal liability to the company and the issue whether the plaintiff has standing to enforce any liability which might be disclosed. It seems to me that the procedure for the determination of the issue of *locus standi* ought to be determined in each individual case according to what appears to be just and convenient in the circumstances of the case.

A similarly robust approach to *Foss* v. *Harbottle* was taken by Megarry J in *Estmanco*.[33] He declared that whatever fraud on a minority might mean 'it is wide enough to cover the present case, and that if it is not, it should now be made wide enough'.

A few years before the *Prudential* case, it will be recalled that Templeman J's memorable decision in *Daniels* v. *Daniels* was widely approved.[34] Attention has already been drawn to the innovative way in which the issue of 'fraudulent transaction' was handled on an interlocutory application to strike out. It is true that neither of these English cases raised issues of *de facto* wrongdoer control. The issue was the nature of the alleged wrongs and not the degree of control exercised by the wrongdoer. If flexibility (in the interest of disposing of artificial technicality) can be

---

[30] See, e.g. *North West Transportation Co. Ltd* v. *Beatty* (1887) LR 12 App Cas 589 (PC); and *Hogg* v. *Cramphorn Ltd* [1967] Ch 254.

[31] *Russell* v. *Wakefield Waterworks* (1875) LR 20 Eq 474; *Heyting* v. *Dupont* [1964] 1 WLR 843 (CA).

[32] (1982) 6 ACLR 791 at 794–8. In Australia, the common law has now been replaced by a statutory derivative action. See, as to the then draft Australian legislation, Law Commission, *Shareholder Remedies: A Consultation Paper* (Law Commission Consultation Paper No. 142, Stationery Office, 1996), paras. 16.27–16.34 and Appendix F at pp. 241–3.

[33] *Estmanco (Kilner House) Ltd* v. *Greater London Council* [1982] 1 WLR 2.

[34] [1978] Ch 406.

employed for one aspect of the 'fraud on a minority' concept, why not in respect of the others? Unless, that is, there are special policy factors that apply only to listed pls, where *de jure* control is unlikely to exist.

What shape might a recast procedure take? A perceptive compromise was well framed by Professor Sealy[35] over a decade ago in these words:

It would surely not be difficult to devise a compromise procedure which allowed the plaintiff an opportunity to advance evidence, and the court to hear it, devoted purely to settling whether there was a *prima facie* case to allow a full scale action to be brought. There is no reason why such an issue should be allowed to be debated for over thirty days. But to make such a system work properly the judges would have to be prepared to break with tradition and play a more interventionist part not unlike that assumed at times by judges of the commercial court. As it is, the court does conduct at least one *prima facie* investigation, and sometimes two, but only for the purpose of answering questions *indirectly* related to the *real* one (which is whether the complaint is one that the court ought in duty to hear), and only under the self-imposed constraint that it must reach a decision without evidence. There is more than this to be said for a system under which the court would allow at least part of a case to be heard before it made even a preliminary decision about it.

In some Australian decisions the court has been even bolder in rejecting the restrictions imposed by the English Court of Appeal in the *Prudential* case. In *Biala Ltd* v. *Malina Holdings*,[36] Ipp J (in the Supreme Court of Western Australia) had no hesitation in applying what has traditionally been termed the 'fifth' exception to *Foss* v. *Harbottle* in circumstances where the 'fourth' exception (fraud on a minority) was not applicable. The judge found that neither 'wrongdoer control' nor a 'fraudulent' breach of directors' duties had been established.[37] He held, however, that the circumstances justified the application of the 'fifth' exception. It relied on the well-known *dicta* from *Russell* v. *Wakefield Waterworks*[38] to *Heyting* v. *Dupont*.[39] In the words of Jenkins LJ in *Edwards* v. *Halliwell*:[40] 'the rule is not an inflexible one and will be relaxed when necessary in the interests of justice'. The strictures of the court of Appeal in *Prudential*[41] were firmly brushed aside. Ipp J referred to the Court of Appeal's own observations that 'it would not be proper for us to express any concluded view on the proper scope of the exceptions to the rule in *Foss* v. *Harbottle*'.[42]

---

[35] See Sealy, 'The Problems of Standing, Pleading and Proof in Corporate Litigation' in B. G. Pettet (ed.), *Company Law in Change* (Stevens & Sons, 1987), p. 13.

[36] (1993) 11 ACLR 785. See further *Dempster* v. *Biala Pty Ltd* (1989) 15 ACLR 191 (Full Court of Western Australia). See also *McLelland* v. *Hullett* (1992) 1 SA 456 (LD Durban and Coast).

[37] (1993) 11 ACLR 785 at 840–4.   [38] (1875) LR 20 Eq 474.

[39] [1964] 1 WLR 847.   [40] [1952] All ER 1064 at 1067.   [41] [1982] 1 Ch 204.

[42] *Ibid.* at 221. See also *ibid.* at 220, where the judgment explained why 'this court cannot on this appeal decide the scope of the exception' to the rule in *Foss* v. *Harbottle*.

Ipp J then observes: 'Even subject to this caveat, their views concerning the fifth exception were tentative.'[43] He then found other indications of 'the lack of finality' of the Court of Appeal's views. After reviewing other Australian decisions,[44] the judge then felt able to come to the conclusion that the court should not shrink from determining whether 'the justice of the case should allow a shareholder to proceed with a derivative action. Equity is concerned with substance and not form and it was contrary to principle to require wronged minority shareholders to bring themselves within the boundaries of well-recognised exceptions and to deny jurisdiction even where an unjust or inconsistent result may otherwise ensue.'

Procedural reform: the Civil Procedure Rules as amended

As Professor Gower and others had long argued, there is a need for reform at the purely procedural level. What was needed was a specific revision of the Rules of the Supreme Court to cope with the real needs of the derivative action rather than continuing to typecast it as a form of shareholders' representative action. This could be done, as Gower contends, either 'by rule of court or a practice direction'.[45]

Knox J in Smith v. Croft, while not going as far as counsel for the plaintiff in calling the existing procedure 'a shambles',[46] described it as having 'unsatisfactory features, not least the length of time taken'. He also indicated that, while the onus of establishing that his case falls within the exceptions to Foss v. Harbottle should continue to be placed on the plaintiff, the onus of establishing whether the company is likely to succeed if the action is brought should not rest on the plaintiff. It might be more appropriate to put 'the onus on the defendants to establish that the case is effectively unarguable'. Knox J (like Walton J in the Wallersteiner application in Smith v. Croft) was firmly of the opinion that, unlike the existing confused procedure, the two applications on the issues of locus standi and the Wallersteiner order should for common sense reasons be heard together.

It is not suggested that a judge in the English Chancery Division is likely to take the vigorous approach that has been taken to the Prudential case in some Australian decisions.[47] Nevertheless, the task of the court here

---

[43] (1993) 11 ACLR 785 at 849.

[44] See Scarel Pty Ltd v. City Loan and Credit Card Pty Ltd (No. 2) (1988) 12 ACLR 730; Campbell v. Kitchen & Sons Ltd and Brisbane Soap Company (1910) 12 CLR 55; and Hawkesbury Development Co. Ltd v. Landmark Finance Pty Ltd [1969] 2 NSWR 787 at 789.

[45] See Sir Jack Jacobs' comment on Order 15, rule 12 in Supreme Court Practice, para. 15/12/9. See L. C. B. Gower (ed.), Gower's Principles of Modern Company Law (5th ed., London, Sweet & Maxwell, 1992), p. 660.

[46] Smith v. Croft (No. 2) [1988] Ch 114 at 189–96.   [47] See pp. 30–1 above.

may be made easier by the general reform of civil procedure heralded by the Woolf Report.[48] This may now provide the courts with new judicial techniques for resolving the factual issues relating to the *locus standi* of plaintiff shareholders in derivative proceedings.

Since a procedural reform first introduced in 1994 as Order 15, rule 12A, the court has been given a range of procedural powers that should enable it to be more flexible in handling derivative proceedings – including the issue of *de facto* control in public listed companies. Even if there is some delay in implementing the Law Commission's Report on shareholder remedies proposing a new statutory derivative action, the current 'judicial reform' of the system of civil procedure may have removed many of the past artificial barriers to derivative litigation.

The same elaborately formulated provisions of Order 15, rule 12A which were preserved in a Schedule to the Civil Procedure Rules 1998,[49] have now been recast in a much simpler form by the Civil Procedure (Amendment) Rules 2000.[50] Both sets of rules advanced the time when the court would decide whether leave to bring a derivative action should be granted. In most cases, this application will be heard by a master rather than a High Court judge. The new Part 19, rule 9 applies to derivative claims. These are simply described as arising where a company is alleged to be entitled to claim a remedy, and a claim is made by one or more members of the company.[51] It is provided that the company must be made a defendant to the claims. After the claim form has been issued, the claimant must apply to the court for permission to continue the claim.[52] The application to the court for leave to proceed must be 'supported by written evidence'.[53] The defendant must have been served with this written evidence in support of the application together with the claim form and the application notice.[54]

If the court gives the claimant permission to continue the claim, the time within which the defence must be filed is fourteen days after the date when the permission is given, or such period as the court may specify.

---

[48] *Access to Justice: An Interim Report to the Lord Chancellor on the Civil Justice System in England and Wales* (HMSO, 1995); and *Access to Justice: Final Report* (HMSO, 1996). See now the Civil Procedure Rules 1998 (SI 1998 No. 3132). See Chapter 3 below.

[49] Civil Procedure Rules 1998, Schedule 1 at pp. 162–3.

[50] SI 2000 No. 221. These rules came into force on 2 May 2000. See *ibid.*, rule 1.

[51] See Civil Procedure Rules 1998, Schedule 1, Part 19, rule 9(1). This also applies to derivative claims on behalf of any incorporated body or trade union.

[52] No other step may then be taken in the proceedings except for the service of the documents prescribed by rule 9(5) or with the leave of the court.

[53] These documents must be served on the defendant within the period within which the claim form must be served and, in any event, at least fourteen days before the court is to deal with the application: rule 9(5).

[54] Rule 9(6).

Provision is made for the court to make costs indemnity orders.[55] It has been argued by a practitioner,[56] that the new procedure makes it much too easy for claimants to gain permission to continue derivative claims. This, it is argued, is because permission is given at far too early a stage simply on the basis of 'written evidence' from the claimant. This evidence on behalf of the claimant will simply assert the plaintiff's allegations as to the nature of the company's claim and the claimant's right to litigate derivatively. The whole point of the new permission procedure is to exclude the defendant raising a proper defence at this stage. However, the defendant's witness statement is likely to contest fiercely the allegation made by the claimant. The defendant's counsel is likely to endeavour to turn the permission application into as fierce a contest as possible. It would seem that in such applications the nature of the procedure will favour the applicant.[57] It would also seem that the legal uncertainty surrounding the notions of both 'wrongdoer control' and 'fraud on the company' in practice have the effect of discouraging the master hearing the application from refusing permission.[58]

The suggestion[59] that the problem of *de facto* control could be solved by the master's tentative approach favouring the claimant under the new procedure seems more doubtful. In the case of a listed public company, where the stakes are very high and the corporate defendants' pockets very deep, a request for a hearing before a High Court judge, and if necessary an appeal to the Court of Appeal, would seem all too likely. Thus all the traditional law on wrongdoer control will come into play. Even if the derivative claim is allowed to proceed, it is difficult to see how these issues will not be raised later at trial or on appeal. The simplified terminology of CPR Part 19, rule 9(4) does not enable a confident answer to be given to the question of how far the *Foss* v. *Harbottle* issue is finally resolved by permitting the derivative claimant to go ahead.

There is clearly concern in some areas of the corporate bar that derivative claims will have too ready access to full trial. An argument can be made for the defendant company resisting applications for costs indemnity orders under Part 19, rule 9(7).[60] There may also be a case for

---

[55] Rule 9(7).

[56] See Reed, 'Derivative Claims' (2000) 21 *Company Lawyer* 156.

[57] It would seem that the court's power under Part 3, rule 1 of the Civil Procedure Rules 1998 to adjourn the application for the filing of further evidence, the cross-examination of witnesses, and the disclosure of documents are not in practice invoked at this stage.

[58] See Reed, 'Derivative Claims' (2000) 21 *Company Lawyer* 156 at 156–7.

[59] *Ibid.*, p. 157. The further suggestion that derivative claims will tend to replace section 459 petitions seems questionable. Clearly, the new procedure is more flexible than the Law Commission's proposed reforms. See *ibid.*, p. 159.

[60] See *ibid.*, p. 158. The restrictive approach taken by Walton J in *Smith* v. *Croft (No. 1)* [1986] BCLC 207 might be adopted by the court.

making a cross-application for a security for costs order under section 726 of the Companies Act 1985. Such a cross-application might be justified where the claimant in the derivative claim is impecunious and the 'real' defendant fears that in the event of the whole claim ultimately failing (i.e. in a claim funded by the company under a costs indemnity order) the claimant will not be able to pay the costs. Here the company should be given security.[61]

Even before the Civil Procedure Rules were brought into force, the Law Commission's Consultation Paper on shareholder remedies designed the new statutory remedy in the light of the case management powers set out in the Woolf Report.[62] The Consultation Paper discussed the 'case management of derivative actions' and proposed that the grant of leave to proceed (in the proposed new statutory remedy) should normally occur in the context of a case management conference.[63]

An imaginative use of the now amended Civil Procedure Rules,[64] in the case of a listed plc, should help to solve the issue of wrongdoer control without having to resort to the vast expense, delay and questionable value of a shareholders' extraordinary general meeting. Other characteristic features of the common law derivative action are still derived from the earlier case law. It has long been recognised, if not by that name, as a distinct type of shareholders' action to enforce corporate rights to recover damages or property belonging to the company. It is brought by the plaintiffs 'on behalf of themselves and all the other shareholders of the company except the defendants'. The reason the action takes this form is that the minority shareholder is not in a position to see that the action is brought in the name of the company itself to enforce the company's rights.[65] Although the action is brought for the benefit of the company, it must be joined as nominal defendant together with the real defendants. No specific relief should be sought against the company and 'what is recovered cannot be paid to the plaintiff representing the minority, but must go to the coffers of the company'.[66]

---

[61] *Ibid.* As to section 726, see *Gore-Browne on Companies* (Jordans, looseleaf), para. 28.11.2.

[62] *Access to Justice: Final Report* (HMSO, 1996).

[63] See *ibid.*, para. 17.6. See also *ibid.*, Part 2; and *ibid.*, Part 6 and para. 6.7. See further Chapter 3 at p. 71 below.

[64] See the discussion above of the Civil Procedure Rules 1998, Part 19, rule 19.9, as amended by the Civil Procedure (Amendment) Rules 2000.

[65] See *Beattie* v. *Beattie Ltd and Beattie* [1938] Ch 708 at 718 *per* Greene MR. See also *Burland* v. *Earle* [1902] AC 83 at 93 *per* Lord Davey.

[66] See *Spokes* v. *Grosvenor Hotel Co.* [1897] 2 QB 124 at 128–9 (CA). See also *Prudential Assurance Co. Ltd* v. *Newman Industries Ltd (No. 2)* [1987] Ch 204 (CA); and *Heron International* v. *Lord Grade* [1983] BCLC 244 (CA).

In a derivative action the plaintiff shareholder can pursue wrongs to the company before he became a member,[67] but may not pursue a derivative action after he ceased to be a member.[68] Derivative litigation must be conducted in good faith. If the plaintiff minority shareholder has participated in the wrongful act of which he complains, his conduct will debar him from pursuing this type of action.[69] Further, such an action must be brought genuinely in the interests of the company and not for the benefit of a rival company which has fostered the litigation and indemnified the litigant against costs.[70]

As a general rule, a derivative action should not be combined with a claim for a wrong done to a shareholder personally. In appropriate circumstances, however, leave may be granted to join the two causes of action.[71]

Funding derivative actions: costs indemnity orders

In *Wallersteiner* v. *Moir*,[72] the Court of Appeal, which generally took a pro-active approach to derivative actions, instituted a new procedure to assist a minority shareholder in financing such proceedings. The Court of Appeal recognised the right of a minority shareholder, who has commenced a derivative action, to an indemnity order in respect of his or her costs. This application to the court was held to be closely analogous to the indemnity to which a trustee is entitled in respect of proceedings on behalf of the trust property or in execution of the trust.[73] Fundamentally, the right to a costs indemnity order will depend on whether the minority shareholders acted in good faith and reasonably in bringing the proceedings. The Court of Appeal in *Wallersteiner* modelled the procedure for the application to claim the order on that already established in the case of a trustee.[74]

Since the procedural reform of the derivative action, there will no longer be the difficulties formerly experienced in a separate application for *locus standi* to proceed and an application for a costs indemnity order. Both issues can be dealt with together under the Civil Procedure (Amendment)

---

[67] *Seaton* v. *Grant* (1867) LR 2 Ch App 45.
[68] *Birch* v. *Sullivan* [1957] 1 WLR 124. The court may then allow another member to be substituted as plaintiff.
[69] *Nurcombe* v. *Nurcombe* [1984] BCLC 557 (CA).
[70] *Forrest* v. *Manchester, Sheffield and Lincolnshire Rly* (1861) 4 De GF & J 126; *Barrett* v. *Duckett* [1995] 1 BCLC 245 (CA).
[71] See *Stroud* v. *Lawson* [1898] 2 QB 44 (CA) and *Cooke* v. *Cooke* [1997] 2 BCLC 28. See p. 58 below as to the relation between derivative and 'direct' action.
[72] [1975] QB 273.   [73] *Hardoon* v. *Belilios* [1901] AC 118 (HL).
[74] See *Wallersteiner* v. *Moir (No. 2)* [1975] QB 373 at 404 *per* Buckley LJ. See *Re Beddoe Downes & Cottam* [1897] 1 Ch 551 as to trustees.

Rules 2000.[75] Although originally such applications were *ex parte*, the procedure has changed.[76]

In *Wallersteiner* v. *Moir*, the Court of Appeal excluded the possibility of legal aid in derivative actions.[77] In any event, legal aid funding would not now be available in such civil proceedings. In most types of civil proceedings, legal aid has now been replaced by the new system of conditional fee agreements regulated under the Courts and Legal Services Act 1990 by provisions brought into force by subsequent statutory instruments.[78] Such agreements can now be used generally in civil proceedings seeking to recover a monetary judgment. The plaintiff has to seek insurance to cover the defendant's legal costs in the event of losing. The plaintiff's legal expenses are met by his or her legal advisers, who, in the event of winning the case, are to be reimbursed from an agreed proportion of the funds recovered by the successful judgment.[79]

While this system has considerable attractions in 'direct' shareholder actions (or a petition under section 459 of the Companies Act 1985)[80] seeking a monetary judgment, it would seem that conditional fee agreements cannot be employed in a derivative action. This issue will be further considered in Chapter 3 in the context of the proposed statutory derivative action.[81] The problem is a requirement common to both the common law derivative action and its proposed statutory successor. In both cases the proceeds of a successful action must accrue to the company alone. This would seem to rule out the use of conditional fee agreements to fund derivative suits. It would require creative judicial 'law-making' to interpret the diversion of funds to the plaintiffs' legal adviser as not amounting to a breach of the general rule. The counter argument is that it is simply a realistic way in the modern context for financing derivative litigation which ultimately, if successful, benefits the company. A more cautious judicial approach is perhaps to be expected in view of the generally negative approach taken to such proceedings. In the case of the existing common law derivative action, it may perhaps be easier to reinterpret existing case law than it would be under the Law Commission's present proposals.[82]

---

[75] See SI 2000 No. 221.

[76] Compare *Wallersteiner* v. *Moir (No. 2)* [1975] QB 373 with *Smith* v. *Croft (No. 1)* [1986] BCLC 207. See *Gore-Brown on Companies*, para. 28.9.1.

[77] See [1975] QB at 400–1 *per* Buckley LJ.

[78] See now the Conditional Fee Agreements Order 1998 (SI 1998 No. 1860). See further the Civil Procedure Rules 1998, rule 48.9.

[79] See generally Underwood, *No Win No Fee* (CLT Professional Publishing, 1998); Napier and Bawdon, *Conditional Fees: A Survival Guide* (Law Society, 1995); and the Access to Justice Act 1999. See also *The Ethics of Conditional Fee Agreements* (Society for Advanced Legal Studies, January 2001).

[80] See p. 59 below.   [81] See p. 83 below.

[82] See the draft section 458A(1) in Appendix A of the Consultation Paper.

The derivative action in the United States

The American version of the Foss v. Harbottle rule

The American version of the *Foss* v. *Harbottle* rule is somewhat unhappily termed 'the requirement of demand'. It is often described as a condition precedent to a minority shareholders' action to enforce corporate rights. Such actions were logically termed, long before the terminology was adopted in England, 'derivative actions'. As the American rule developed, it required two conditions to be met by a minority shareholder: there must be a 'demand', first, upon the board of directors to take proceedings on behalf of the corporation, followed by another similar 'demand' addressed to the general body of shareholders (where the board reject the demand made upon them). In each case, the minority shareholder must aver in his or her pleadings either that he or she has made these requests, one or both of which has been wrongfully refused, or, alternatively, that it would be futile in the circumstances to make one or both of these 'demands'. If the plaintiff could not make these averments at the outset of the trial, the action is barred.

As in English law,[83] the source of the modern rule restricting minority actions is to be found in early-nineteenth-century decisions. The American courts began to evolve a rule (restricting minority shareholder actions) of their own devising some years before *Foss* v. *Harbottle* was decided. One important difference was that the American courts were dealing with corporations and not overgrown partnerships. This was because 'general corporation laws' were introduced much earlier than Gladstone's Act of 1844.[84]

There is no evidence that the American courts at this period were influenced by the rather similar rule that was being developed by the English courts for unincorporated joint stock companies. Neither judges nor counsel seem to have known, or at any rate saw any reason to cite, English decisions like *Carlen* v. *Drury*.[85] The most plausible explanation is that English decisions on the standing of the minority were concerned with principles of partnership law and not of corporation law and on that account were not brought to the attention of the American courts.[86]

The early American cases were concerned entirely with what came to be called 'derivative' actions. The courts were dealing with waste or

---

[83] See Chapter 1, p. 2 above.
[84] 7 & 8 Vict. c. 110. New York, for example, had a 'general corporation law' for manufacturing companies as early as 1811. Some states had 'general acts of incorporation' for insurance or utility companies even before 1800. See J. S. Davies, *Essays in the Earlier History of American Corporations* (1917), vol. II, pp. 8 and 16–17.
[85] (1812) V & B 154 at 159.
[86] See further Boyle, (1962) 25 *Modern Law Review* 317 at 320–3.

misapplication of corporate funds by the officers or agents of the company. Such a suit must nominally be instituted by the innocent members of the board on their own initiative or at the request of the shareholders in general meeting. Such actions were corporate actions in the sense of being brought in the corporate name. On the other hand, the court (exercising Chancery jurisdiction) would never permit a wrong to go unredressed for the sake of form. An action would lie if those who wronged the corporation were in control of it or if the wrongdoer were acting in collusion with them.[87] Increasing emphasis was laid on the need to exhaust any remedy within the corporation. As a rule, the minority must first demand from the directors redress for their grievances before coming to court.

The early American authorities do not expound the principle of non-interference in matters of internal regulation which from the first characterised the English rule. Moreover, it had not yet occurred to the American courts to examine the majority shareholders' power to ratify in the context of minority actions to remedy wrongs to their corporation.

In 1870, an important case was decided which clarified the American law. The decision of the Massachusetts Supreme Court in *Brewer* v. *Boston Theatre*[88] laid the foundation of the twentieth-century American law on the 'requirement of demand'. For the first time it is clearly stated that separate 'demands' must be made on the board of directors and on the body of shareholders; but where fraudulent conduct or *ultra vires* acts are the ground of complaint both forms of demand are 'excused'. It is not a matter of chance that, in the earliest leading American decision to draw extensively upon English material, the effect of the majority's right to ratify minority action for wrongs to the company should have been considered for the first time.[89] However, the English *Foss* v. *Harbottle* principle underwent, in the process of reception by the American courts, a change which still characterises the American rule. The majority's power to ratify is made to explain the need for a 'demand' on the shareholders; whereas the principle that the corporation is the proper plaintiff in any action to enforce its rights is held to require a separate 'demand' upon the board of directors.

The US Supreme Court in *Hawes* v. *Oakland*[90] completed the re-statement of the basic principles of the American rule in their 'modern' form. This decision was even more strongly influenced by English law.

---

[87] See e.g. *Robinson* v. *Smith*, 3 Paige 222 at 234 (NY Ch., 1832).

[88] 104 Mass 738 (1870).

[89] The American courts were well aware of the limits to be placed upon the majority's power to ratify as it affected other forms of minority rights enforceable by 'direct' action.

[90] 104 US 450 at 460 (1882). On the federal jurisdictional background to this decision, and the embodiment of its conclusions in rule 23(b) of the Federal Rules of Civil Procedure, see Moore, *Federal Practice* (2nd ed., 1948), section 23.15.2.

Justice Miller, who delivered the judgment for the Supreme Court, came nearer to the English rule than an American court has ever done since. Nonetheless, even though Justice Miller was under the impression that he was stating a doctrine 'not different in any material respect from that found in other English and American courts', there were still striking differences. Thus there is no attempt to deduce from earlier cases a substantive rule prohibiting minority shareholders' actions in general terms. A policy restricting such actions is implicit in the argument but their policy is not explained or justified. Furthermore, the English rule, stricter though it was and is in all other respects, by this time no longer required[91] that the plaintiff comply with the formality of making any form of 'demand'. Perhaps the most radical difference between the two rules is that the American 'requirement of demand' does not apply to shareholders' action to enforce their own rights under statute, the charter or byelaws. It is confined to derivative actions for wrongs to the corporation. In contrast, under English law every minority shareholders' action must be brought under one or other of the 'exceptions' to the *Foss v. Harbottle* rule.

Subsequent development of the 'demand' rule

Twentieth-century developments in the formulation of the requirement of demand on the board of directors greatly facilitated the bringing of derivative suits. It will be seen later that in the closing decades of the last century a new and much stricter doctrinal approach was taken. Earlier in that century, a demand would be excused altogether if the plaintiff could allege either a domination or control of the board of directors by the defendant wrongdoer, or even a collusion with them by a majority of the board. Such collusion could be shown even though the majority were in good faith and not themselves in breach of fiduciary duty.[92]

When a demand on the board to bring proceedings was not excused, the plaintiff could still challenge the board's refusal to litigate where a 'wrongful refusal' could be shown. The court would hold a refusal by the board to adopt a derivative suit 'wrongful', not only where it was made in bad faith, but also where there was inexcusable neglect in protecting the interests of the corporation. In some jurisdictions, most notably that of New York, an even more liberal rule was followed. Where, in the pleadings, a sound corporate cause of action was alleged the board, having had an opportunity to decide whether or not to adopt the suit, could not

---

[91] See, for example, *MacDougall v. Gardiner* (1975) 1 ChD 13 at 25.
[92] See e.g. *Hill v. Wallace*, 259 US 44 at 61 (1922).

further bar a derivative action.[93] The directors were not allowed simply to assert that it was not expedient in the interests of the corporation to bring the action.

The abuse of derivative suits

It was the laxity of the 'requirement of demand', as it evolved, that enabled the derivative action to be abused and for the notorious 'strike suit' to become common. The 'strike suit' was based on a corporate cause of action of dubious or questionable merit, whose real object was to obtain an out-of-court settlement which benefited only the plaintiff and his lawyer. The corporation had, of course, to provide the financial settlement at the behest of directors who might wish to avoid the embarrassment of litigation in open court. 'Security for expenses' legislation,[94] which has long existed in some jurisdictions, did not prevent a thriving industry in often unmeritorious derivative litigation. It was in this context that boards of directors in public listed corporations and their legal advisers developed a new strategy. The device they constructed was the 'special litigation committee' to protect publicly held corporations from what was characterised as speculative and possibly harmful litigation which did not have the true interests of the corporation in mind.[95]

In *Gall* v. *Exxon*[96] (a case in the federal courts applying New York law), the special litigation committee was upheld on the basis of the 'business judgment rule' – a fundamental principle of American corporate law. The effect of *Gall* was to transmute a discussion in court of the merits of the plaintiffs' derivative suit into a discussion of the *bona fides* of the exercise of business judgment by the special litigation committee. This related to their decision to discontinue the derivative suit by the exercise of the board's general power to manage the affairs of the corporation. The appointment of a special committee rapidly became the standard response by the board of a publicly held corporation when faced with a derivative action.

---

[93] See *Epstein* v. *Schenck*, 35 NYS 2d 909 at 981 (Sup. Ct, 1939); *Groel* v. *United Electric Co. of New Jersey*, 70 NJ Eq 616, 61 A 1061 at 1064 (Ch., 1905).

[94] For the operation of such legislation where the 'strike suit' was still in its prime, see Baker and Company, *Corporation Cases and Materials* (3rd ed., 1959), pp. 674–82. Here, the texts of section 61B of the New York General Corporation Law and § 834 of the Californian Corporation Code are given. See *ibid.*, pp. 717–19 on the significance of 'counsel fee' awards out of money or property recovered for the corporation. These awards reimburse the plaintiffs for attorneys' fees and litigation expenses.

[95] *Gall* v. *Exxon*, 418 F Supp 508 (United States District Court, SDNY, 1976).

[96] *Gall* v. *Exxon*, 418 F Supp 508 (United States District Court, SDNY, 1976). The imposition of a demanding and strict standard of care on 'outside' directors played a significant part in these developments. See *Smith* v. *Van Gorkens*, 488 A 2d 858 (Sup. Ct Del., 1985).

In a further important development, the courts of Delaware[97] attempted to restore to some degree the right of minority shareholders to pursue well-founded derivative suits. These Delaware decisions did not question the legitimate role of the special litigation committee (or indeed of an independent board of directors) and their right to rely on the business judgment principle. However, these cases applied the courts' power of judicial review of the discretion exercised on behalf of the corporation, based on a standard more exacting than the criteria of independence and good faith indicated in *Exxon*.

In *Zapata Corp.* v. *Maldonado*,[98] the Delaware Supreme Court established a 'two-step' test for the exercise of the courts' power of judicial review. This substantive judicial review applied whenever the requirement of demand was excused. In the cases where the minority shareholder is required to make a demand and it is refused, the board's (or litigation committee's) decision not to bring a derivative action will be upheld so long as it satisfies the basic standards of the business judgment rule. Where a demand is excused, an independent board or a special litigation committee can still determine that the derivative action can be dismissed. In proceedings for judicial review of this exercise of business judgment, the committee can still determine that the derivative action can be dismissed and apply to the court for dismissal. In proceedings for judicial review of this exercise of business judgment, following *Zapata*, the court applies the 'two-step' test. First, the court must inquire into the independence and good faith of the litigation committee (or of the board where no committee is appointed), and review the reasonableness and good faith of its investigation. Secondly, the court must apply its own independent judgment to decide whether the motion to dismiss should be granted.

In a subsequent Delaware decision, *Aronson* v. *Lewis*,[99] the court clarified, for the purposes of invoking the two-step approach in *Zapata*, the circumstances in which a demand will be excused. Here the court, in order to determine the futility of demand, must decide, on the basis of the particularised facts alleged in the pleadings, if a reasonable doubt is created as to whether the directors or the litigation committee are disinterested and independent. The court must also determine whether the challenged transaction was, in other respects, the product of a valid exercise of business judgment. The court does not assume that the transaction with the

---

[97] Delaware corporations law, of course, governs very many publicly held corporations which choose to incorporate in that state.

[98] 430 A 2d 779 (Sup. Ct Del., 1981).

[99] 437 A 805 (Sup. Ct Del., 1984). See also *Re Walt Disney Company's Derivative Litigation*, 731 A 2d 342 (Del. Ch., 1997).

corporation (impugned by the plaintiff) requires collective steps by the board. However, the alleged wrong is substantively reviewed against the factual background alleged in the complaint. Later cases indicated what amounts to well-pleaded claims of fraud, bad faith or self-dealing in the challenged transaction. Clearly, diversion of substantial corporate assets will be significant.[100] The undoubted effect of the Delaware approach to the special litigation committee is greatly to curb the use of derivative suits.

In cases in federal courts based on diversity of citizenship jurisdiction, the courts applied the relevant state law as to the making of a demand in a derivative action and as to what excuses a demand. The state law is that of the state of incorporation. In general procedural terms, rule 23.1 of the Federal Rules of Procedure applies.[101]

The American Law Institute's solution

What has come to be known as the Delaware demand rule has been criticised because of its procedural complexity and its tendency to prolong litigation. The Delaware rule can also be a trap for the unwary.[102] The American Law Institute, in its Corporate Governance project,[103] sought to provide a more coherent approach. A key part of its proposed approach was to insist on a demand on the board in most circumstances. In contrast to the Delaware rule, substantive judicial review would be located, procedurally speaking, in the corporation's motion to dismiss the derivative action.

Under the American Law Institute's model, in the case of most breaches of the director's duty of loyalty, the derivative action will be dismissed if the court finds that the board (or the litigation committee) was adequately informed under the circumstances, and had reasonably determined that dismissal was in the best interests of the corporation. This must be based on grounds that 'warrant reliance'. A much tougher approach is taken if

---

[100] Compare *Grobow* v. *Perct*, 539 A 2d 180 (Sup. Ct Del., 1998) with *Heineman* v. *Datapoint Corp.*, 611 A 2d 950 (Sup. Ct Del., 1992). See further *Ryan* v. *Tapps Energy Oil*, 709 A 2d 682 (Del. Ch., 1996); *Jackson National Life Insurance* v. *Kennedy*, 741 A 2d 377 (Del. Ch., 1999); and *Parnes* v. *Bally Entertainments*, 772 A 2d 249 (Sup. Ct Del., 1999).

[101] See e.g. *Garber* v. *Lego*, 11 F 2d 1197 (3rd Cir., 1993) applying the law of Pennsylvania; and *Stepack* v. *Addison*, 20 F 2d 398 (11th Cir., 1994) applying the law of Delaware. See further *Kamen* v. *Kemper Financial Services*, 500 US 90 (US Sup. Ct, 1991) and *Re Silicon Graphics Inc. Securities Litigation*, 183 F 2d 92 (9th Cir., 1999). As to litigation based on a federal statute, see *First Hartford Corp. Pension Plan and Trust* v. *US*, 194 F 2d 1279 (USCA Federal Cir., 1999).

[102] See Coffee, 'New Myths and Old Realities: The American Law Institute Faces the Derivative Action' (1993) 48 *Business Law Review* 1407 at 1414.

[103] See Part VII, Chapter 1, paras. 7.012–7.10 (1994).

the plaintiff can establish that dismissal would involve the retention of a 'significant improper benefit'. Where the following three alternative criteria are involved, the court should not dismiss the action. These are: (i) that the defendant retaining the benefit was in control of the corporation alone or with others; (ii) it may be shown that the benefit was obtained as a result of a knowing and material representation (or omission) or other fraudulent action; or (iii) if the improper benefit was obtained without advance authorisation or requisite ratification by disinterested directors or disinterested shareholders.

The standard of judicial review proposed by the American Law Institute is more relaxed where the gravamen of the claim is a breach of the duty of care, and this does not involve a known or culpable breach of law. Here the action will be dismissed unless the board's, or the litigation committee's determination fails to satisfy the general requirements of the business judgment rule.

Although the American Law Institute's proposals have been adopted in some states,[104] it has met with considerable criticism from corporate law scholars for allowing too much interference by the court under the guise of judicial review.[105] Critics tend to prefer the Delaware approach. The changes introduced into the Model Business Corporation Act by the Committee on Corporate Laws in 1989[106] have a much less demanding standard of judicial review. This model has been followed in a number of states,[107] although it has not been universally adopted.

For large, publicly held American corporations, Delaware law on the judicial review of the special litigation committee will very commonly be the applicable law. While giving little encouragement to derivative suits, it still allows legitimate shareholder grievances to be properly ventilated. The work of the special litigation committee will be the subject of substantive judicial review whenever dishonest or self-interested breaches of duty are alleged. Procedural clarity, and clearly defined standards of review, make the employment of derivative proceedings a genuine possibility. The present state of the English common law derivative action is much less satisfactory, even in cases where serious fraud is alleged by a minority shareholder in a public listed company.

---

[104] E.g. *Coker v. Mikalauskas*, 547 Pa 600, 692 A 2d 1042 (Supreme Court of Pennsylvania, 1997).

[105] See e.g. Larry R. Fischel and Michael Bradley, 'The Role of Liability Rules and the Derivative Suit in Corporate Law' (1986) 71 *Cornell Law Review* 261.

[106] See subchapter D of Chapter 7 at paras. 7.40 *et seq.*

[107] See Hamilton, *Cases and Materials on Corporations* (7th edn, 1998), pp. 748–9.

Demand on the shareholders

A further precondition to bringing a derivative action was, until recent times,[108] that a demand be made on the shareholders as a body to decide whether the action should be proceeded with or abandoned. This might come into play where the demand on the board of directors was excused or had been wrongfully refused. As a result of developments in recent decades in jurisdictions of major significance in corporate law, this further requirement of demand on the shareholders has been abolished either by statute or by case law.[109]

The percentage of capital solution: France and Germany

French law

The French legislation which governs the *société anonyme* (SA), the broad equivalent of a public company in UK law, makes provision for minority shareholders' actions to enforce the civil liability of directors and officers. The legislation makes provision, first, for actions by the company itself and for personal actions by shareholders for losses caused by directors, individually or collectively where the shareholders suffer in their individual capacity.[110] Secondly, specific provision is made for derivative actions by minority shareholders to enforce the civil liability of directors individually or collectively. In contrast with the procedural complexities and obscurities of Anglo-Saxon law, the French equivalent of the *Foss* v. *Harbottle* rule is a threshold of 5 per cent of the share capital.[111] This is lower than the equivalent threshold of 10 per cent in German law.[112] It is clearly a more realistic hurdle to overcome by shareholders acting together. Admittedly, in the case of really large listed companies, even a 5 per cent holding may well prove an insuperable barrier. In this derivative procedure, the company is made a party to the action by serving notice of the proceedings on the company's legal representatives.[113] The statement

---

[108] See p. 41 above.

[109] E.g. California and New York by legislation and Delaware by judicial decision. The federal courts have repeatedly rejected a demand on shareholders in publicly held corporations. See the American Law Institute's Principles of Corporate Governance, Part VII and the comment to rule 703(c).

[110] E.g. an action for fraudulent misrepresentation by directors inducing shareholders to subscribe for additional shares on the basis of false balance sheets.

[111] See Article 245 of Law No. 66-537 and Article 200 of the Decree of 1967.

[112] A 10 per cent threshold has been adopted in the EU draft of the Fifth Company Law Directive as well as in the European Company proposals.

[113] Article 201.

of claim is served on the company. One or more of the minority share-holders (rather than the company's usual 'designated representatives') have control of the proceedings.[114] In such proceedings, any damages must be awarded to the company.

In 1988, a later revision of the original text of Article 200 modified the original 5 per cent threshold in the case of companies with substantial share capital. When the issued capital of a company is larger than FFr5 million in par value, a sliding scale begins to operate which reduces the percentage of shareholding which a minority shareholder must possess in order to bring a derivative action. Where their holding amounts to FFr5 million, they must own 4 per cent of that tranche of capital (i.e. of the first FFr5 million). For the tranche of capital between FFr5 million and FFr50 million the minority must hold 2.5 per cent. If applicable in their particular company, they must hold 1 per cent of the tranche of capital between FFr50 million and FFr100 million. As regards any capital over FFr100 million, they must hold 0.5 per cent.[115]

This realistic and flexible solution to the problem posed by the listed public company (or indeed any large public company) is to be welcomed. It is a matter of regret that the English Law Commission, in its task of reforming the derivative action,[116] did not explore this solution provided by French law.

Another procedural avenue is open to minority shareholders to enforce the civil liability of directors and officers, apart from the 'normal' deriva-tive action under the provisions of Article 200 of the Decree of 1967. This is an action of loss brought by one or more shareholders person-ally to enforce a right vested in the company. This action, known as the *action social exercée ut singuli* is open to any shareholder regardless of the number of shares he or she holds. Despite the apparent attractions of this procedure, it is rarely used in France.[117] This form of procedure in-creases the risks of litigation to the individual shareholders without any compensating advantage in terms of financial benefit. The costs and risks

---

[114] The withdrawal during proceedings of one or more of the shareholders, either because they are no longer shareholders or because they withdraw voluntarily, has no effect on the conduct of the proceedings.

[115] Decree No. 88-56 of 19 January 1988. See also Article 199 inserted by this Decree. This regulates a type of representative action by some shareholders acting on behalf of others. I am indebted for these very brief observations on French law to the advice of Dr Frederique Dahan of the School of Law at the University of Essex.

[116] See Law Commission, *Shareholder Remedies* (Law Commission Report No. 246, Cm 3769, Stationery Office, 1997), discussed in Chapter 3 below. For a broader similar reform in German law, see p. 47 below.

[117] See further Yves Guyon, *Droit des Affaires*, Tome 1, *Droit Commercial Général et Sociétés* (10th ed., Economica, Paris, 1998), sections 462–463. This examines the problems raised by this form of procedure.

of litigation can be shared among a group of minority shareholders acting collectively under Article 200.

The French legislation[118] invalidates any provision in the company's constitution which would require the plaintiff in a derivative action to obtain prior authorisation from the general meeting of shareholders. Nor may the general meeting be summoned to pronounce on the desirability of the action being brought. Furthermore, no resolution passed by a general meeting may release or discharge directors from liability for breach of duty in carrying out their functions.[119]

Thus the whole problem of ratification and ratifiability – which, even in the Law Commission's proposals[120] for reforming the derivative action, imposes major difficulties in English law – has been banished from French law.

German law

The provisions of the German Stock Corporation Act of 1965[121] apply a percentage of shareholding test as a threshold requirement for minority shareholders' actions. It is obviously a higher hurdle to overcome than its French equivalent. The holders of one-tenth of the company's capital may require claims for damages to be brought by the company against members of its board of management or supervisory board for breaches of duty. Article 147(1) of the Stock Corporation Act contemplates that this right to enforce breaches of duty relates to the holding of a shareholders' meeting. The minority's right may be asserted 'if the shareholders' meeting so resolves by simple majority or if a minority, whose aggregate holdings equal or exceed one tenth of the share capital, so requests'. Such a request by a minority must be acted upon only if evidence is furnished that the shareholders who constitute the minority have been holders of shares for not less than three months prior to the date of the shareholders' meeting.

The link between the minority's right to proceed and the holding of a meeting must, in the case of any large public company, present a significant deterrent. The 10 per cent requirement is likewise an extremely difficult hurdle in the case of a large listed company.

However, two consequential provisions in Article 147[122] are 'triggered' by alternative criteria which are not restricted to the 10 per cent of capital test. This is replaced by a monetary amount measured in terms of

---

[118] See Article 246 of the Law of 1966.   [119] *Ibid.*, Article 246(2).

[120] See Chapter 3 below.

[121] See Article 147 of the *Aktiengesetz* 1968, as amended by the Act of 28 October 1994. For a translation see Hans Schroeder and Martin Heidenhain (eds.), *The German Stock Corporation Act* (bilingual edition, CH Beck and Kluwer, 1996).

[122] *Aktiengesetz*, Article 147(2).

par value of the shares. This dual approach applies further to the procedure by which an action for 'compensation of damages' is brought, whether the initial authorisation (under Article 147(1)) is a simple majority resolution or a 10 per cent minority shareholder's request. In either event, the court shall appoint special representatives to assert the claim for damages. This may be done on a motion by the minority shareholders whose holding meets either the test of 10 per cent of total share capital or, alternatively, they hold shares of €1 million in par value terms. The court must appoint such special representative (i.e. persons other than those normally entitled to represent the company) to assert the corporate claim if 'in the opinion of the court such appointment is appropriate for the proper assertion of the claim'.[123] Article 147(3) now provides a new 'substantive' minority shareholder remedy where no claim for compensation under Article 147(1) is brought. Here a lower hurdle for minority litigation has been introduced. On a motion by shareholders whose aggregate holdings equal or exceed 5 per cent of the share capital or whose holdings are worth at least €500,000 in par value, the court shall appoint a special representative provided 'the facts exist which give urgent reason to suspect that improprieties or gross violations of the law or the articles have damaged the company'.

The criteria in the new Article 147(3) are clearly much more satisfactory from a minority shareholder's perspective. It rightly imposes an evidential burden of showing a *prima facie* case of serious corporate wrongdoing, but it is much less demanding than the English rule in *Foss* v. *Harbottle*.

In the case of large listed public companies, the alternative criteria in Article 147(3) possess a realistic flexibility. A complaining minority have the choice between a 5 per cent test or a relatively modest par value holding. Broadly, this follows the criteria of modern French law. It is a solution to the problem posed by public companies that the English Law Commission could with advantage have considered in their proposals to reform the common law derivative action.

There is a further attraction in the German Stock Corporation Act's provisions. It is that it provides for the company to be ordered by the court to bear the costs of the litigation. The court-appointed representatives may request from the company reimbursement for reasonable cash expenses and remuneration of their services. The courts must set the amount of those expenses and remuneration.[124] Where the 'company' proves unsuccessful in the consequent litigation, the minority must

---

[123] *Ibid.*, Article 147.
[124] The court may appoint representatives and set the level of expenses; and such matters are subject to appeal.

reimburse the costs to the company.[125] Where the proceedings are wholly unsuccessful this will include the costs of the court application for appointment of a representative. Such provisions are lacking in the equivalent French legislation, but still involve a larger financial risk than the system of costs indemnity orders under English law.

Appointment of 'special auditors'

Both French and German law afford a further procedural minority remedy. On application to the court, a special auditor may be appointed to examine complaints raised by minority shareholders. In the French legislation governing the *société anonyme*, provision is made for minority shareholders to request the court to appoint auditors acting for the minority (in place of those appointed by the general meeting). The court may also, on a request by the minority, appoint an expert to investigate the management of the company's affairs.[126] In both types of application, shareholders representing at least 10 per cent of the share capital may make such an application.[127]

In the German Stock Corporation Act, the holders of 10 per cent of the company's shares, or of share capital with the par value of €1 million, may request the court to appoint special auditors to investigate the formation or management of the company.[128] The shareholders' meeting also has the right to appoint special auditors by simple majority. The minority shareholders' right to request the court only arises if the shareholders' meeting has rejected a motion to appoint special auditors.[129]

'Direct' shareholders' suits

The terminology employed to describe shareholders' common law claims (or 'actions' in the traditional usage) varies as between various textbook authorities. It will be seen that this is more than a matter of mere nomenclature. Some texts use the term 'personal action'. This is the description adopted by the Law Commission in its reforming work on shareholders'

---

[125] *Aktiengesetz*, Article 147(4).

[126] See Articles 225 and 226 of the Law of 1966 as amended Law No. 84-148 and Law No. 94-679.

[127] As also can the personnel committee, the public prosecutor and, in the case of listed companies, the Stock Exchange Operations Committee.

[128] It also covers 'steps taken on an increase or reduction of share capital'.

[129] *Aktiengesetz*, Article 142. See further, as to the selection of special auditors, Article 143; as to the rights of such auditors on their report, Article 145; and as to the costs of the audit to be borne by the company, Article 147.

remedies.[130] It is also used in the current edition of *Gower's Principles of Modern Company Law*,[131] but is used to discriminate between 'personal, representative, derivative and corporate actions'. This still requires a general term for both personal (or individual) shareholder suits and representative (but non-derivative) suits. There is also a possible area of confusion between 'personal rights' (only one class of direct claim) and 'individual action'.[132] It is possible to avoid this confusion by using the phrase 'shareholders' actions against the company'.[133] It is thought that the terms 'personal' or 'individual' action (or claim) are best avoided, except to describe those shareholder proceedings which are not brought in the representative form. It should be confined to 'direct' claims where the minority shareholder (or small group of such) are the parties of record.

The term 'direct claim' also makes clear that such proceedings are not confined to 'personal' or 'individual' shareholders' rights. It will be seen that shareholders have a limited right to enforce the company's constitution or redress violation of corporate legality. This was recognised under the traditional *ultra vires* and 'illegality' exception to the rule in *Foss* v. *Harbottle*. It will also be seen that certain abuses of power by directors and the violation of due process in passing a resolution in company meetings may be challenged. Such claims are not necessarily linked to any personal or individual right of a complaining shareholder.

Thus the attraction of the general category of 'direct action' as the antithesis of the shareholders' derivative action[134] is that it correctly locates the common denominator among various kinds of non-derivative claim. While these represent a somewhat heterogeneous range of claims, they are all brought directly against the company as true defendant, and they seek a remedy enforceable against the company. This remedy is nearly always an injunction or declaration, but may in some cases be a liquidated sum (e.g. a capital payment due or a dividend declared but not paid).[135]

---

[130] See Consultation Paper, Section A at pp. 8–21; and Law Commission, *Shareholder Remedies* (Law Commission Report No. 246, Cm 3769, Stationery Office, 1997), paras. 6.51. The Law Commission's system of classification is discussed further in Chapter 3 below.

[131] P. L. Davies (ed.), *Gower's Principles of Modern Company Law* (6th ed., London, Sweet & Maxwell, 1997), p. 665.

[132] See *Farrar's Company Law* (3rd ed., Butterworths, 1991), pp. 446–8; and *Pennington's Company Law* (7th ed., Butterworths, 1995), which refers to only 'representative' and 'derivative' actions.

[133] See *Boyle and Birds' Company Law* (3rd ed., Jordans, 1995), para. 5.10.

[134] This is a distinction long made in American law.

[135] Unliquidated claims, for historical reasons connected with capital maintenance, may only be brought in the context of the allotment of shares or for a breach of a shareholder agreement to which the company is a party.

In conclusion, confusion will be best avoided if the term 'direct claim (or action)' is used. Such claims, procedurally speaking, can either be brought by individual shareholders acting in isolation or as a non-derivative suit on behalf of the shareholders as a whole or a class of them.

Categories of direct action

In the discussion which follows, incidental reference will be made to well-established principles of company law relating to the corporate constitution, to shareholders and to membership rights, directors' duties, etc. The issue of concern for present purposes is the *locus standi* of shareholders and, later, the appropriate procedural form of shareholders' direct claims. For a fuller exploration of the substantive company law, which provides the context in which the question of shareholders' rights of access to the courts arises, reference may be had to the standard texts. The categories considered below appear to provide the most illuminating way of subsuming many particular instances in a controversial body of case law into coherent legal principles. Inevitably, some overlap and uncertainty as between the several categories is unavoidable.

Personal or individual rights This is one of the traditional 'exceptions' to the rule in *Foss* v. *Harbottle*. It relates to rights enjoyed by shareholders in respect of their status as members as well as the property rights attaching to their shares. So far as such rights are conferred by the Companies Act 1985 no further discussion is called for. The slightly more controversial question is the extent to which various provisions in the members' contract qualify as actionable personal rights. On orthodox *Foss* v. *Harbottle* principles not every provision in the articles or rule of company law relating to the conduct of shareholders' meetings will have this protection. As was seen in the previous chapter, neither 'internal irregularity' nor 'mere breaches of the articles' give rise to shareholder litigation.

Either in the articles, or implied by law in the contract of association, every shareholder has the following 'personal rights' in addition to those embodied in legislation.[136] He or she is entitled to have their name and shareholding entered on the register of members[137] and can prevent an authorised addition or alteration being made to such an entry.[138] There is a right to vote at meetings,[139] to receive dividends which have been duly

---

[136] See generally *Pennington's Company Law* (7th ed., Butterworths, 1995), p. 866.
[137] *Re British Sugar Refining Co.* (1857) 3 K & J 408.
[138] *Pender* v. *Lushington* (1877) 6 ChD 70.
[139] *Wood* v. *Odessa Waterworks Co.* (1889) 42 ChD 656.

declared or which have become due under the terms of the articles.[140] Any shareholders may exercise pre-emption rights over other members' shares which are conferred by the articles. Every shareholder has a right to have his or her capital repaid in the proper order of priority in the winding up of the company or on a duly authorised reduction of capital.[141] There is also a right to transfer shares.[142] In relation to the conduct of meetings, individual shareholders, in addition to the right to vote, have a right to a reasonable opportunity to speak at meetings[143] and to move amendments to resolutions at meetings.[144]

On the other hand, the concept of mere 'internal irregularity' in respect of the conduct of meetings means that a shareholder cannot restrain directors from acting after their term of office fixed by the articles has expired,[145] and cannot complain if meetings of shareholders are irregularly convened or conducted.[146] The most controversial case in this category is the decision in *MacDougall* v. *Gardiner*[147] that a shareholder may not challenge even a wrongful decision of the chairman of the meeting to refuse to take a poll. This is obviously very difficult to reconcile with the decision in *Pender* v. *Lushington*[148] that the refusal of a chairman to recognise votes attached to shares held by nominee shareholders was an infringement of their personal rights. It may be accepted that on any rational basis these two cases are irreconcilable. Clearly, as Gower observes,[149] there is a contradiction between the proper recognition of the contractual nature of the company's constitution and the traditional policy of non-interference by the courts in the internal affairs of the company. It will be seen below that, while the Law Commission regarded this 'heartland' of *Foss* v. *Harbottle* as beyond its remit, the DTI's proposals, in their consultation paper, *Developing the Framework*, indicates a serious attempt to come to grips with the difficulties self-evident in the case law.[150]

The traditional contention that a mere breach of the articles cannot be the subject of a minority shareholders' suit must be supported in so

---

[140] *Rayfield* v. *Hands* [1960] Ch 1.   [141] *Griffith* v. *Paget* (1877) 5 ChD 894.

[142] *Re Smith Knight & Co., Weston's Case* (1868) 4 Ch App 20.

[143] *Wall* v. *London and Northern Assets Corporation* [1898] 2 Ch 469.

[144] *Henderson* v. *Bank of Australia* (1890) 45 ChD 330.

[145] *Mozeley* v. *Alston* (1847) 1 Ph 790.

[146] *Cotter* v. *National Union of Seamen* [1929] 2 Ch 58 at 70; *Bentley Stevens* v. *Jones* [1974] 1 WLR 638.

[147] (1875) 1 ChD 13.   [148] (1877) 6 ChD 70.

[149] See P. L. Davies (ed.), *Gower's Principles of Modern Company Law* (6th ed., London, Sweet & Maxwell, 1997), p. 662. See further R. J. Smith, 'Minority Shareholders and Corporate Irregularities' (1978) 41 *Modern Law Review* 147.

[150] See p. 55 below.

far as such breaches do not of themselves create an individual or personal shareholders' right. However, it will be seen that other grounds for shareholders' direct claim may coincidentally permit certain breaches of, or departures from, the articles of association to be litigated.

Right to uphold the constitution or corporate legality One of the oldest 'exceptions' to the *Foss* v. *Harbottle* rule is that of 'illegality and *ultra vires*'. As regards 'illegality', this clearly comprehends violations of mandatory requirements of company legislation. In Australia, it has been held that 'illegal' in this context should be understood to mean either 'contrary to company law or so plainly illegal that directors have acted in abuse of their powers'. Where all that is alleged is that the company has engaged in conduct that is contrary to the general law in the sense that it may result, or has resulted, in criminal prosecution of the company, a shareholder will not necessarily have standing (e.g. for a 'technical' offence, or on the basis of legal advice that the conduct was lawful).[151]

It has long been established that a shareholder may seek an injunction to restrain a proposed transaction which is *ultra vires* the company in a direct action.[152] This may occur even where the shareholder does not meet the qualifications to bring a derivative action seeking to recover assets by setting aside a completed *ultra vires* transaction.[153] In the reform of the *ultra vires* doctrine, introduced by the Companies Act 1989 in the form of 'new' section 35 of the Companies Act 1985,[154] minority shareholders' rights of direct action are explicitly preserved by section 35(2). In consequence of the protection afforded to third parties dealing with the company by section 35(1), minority shareholders are no longer able to seek to undo completed transactions. It has been observed[155] that, in the case of large public companies, shareholders are unlikely to have the information to take preventive action in time. In the case of private companies, it may very occasionally be resorted to but other minority remedies are more likely to be used.[156]

The reform of the *Turquand* rule in section 35A (also introduced by the Companies Act 1989) likewise preserves[157] the rights of members to

---

[151] See *Australian Agricultural* v. *Oatmount Pty Ltd* (1992) 8 ACSR 225 (CA of the Northern Territories). Contrast *Wallersteiner* v. *Moir (No. 1)* [1974] 1 WLR 991 (CA).

[152] *Simpson* v. *Westminster Palace Hotel Co.* (1860) 8 HLC 712.

[153] See *Taylor* v. *NUM* [1985] BCLC 237. See further *Mosely* v. *Koffyfontein Mines* [1911] 1 Ch 73 (CA).

[154] See section 108 of the Companies Act 1989. As to the liability of directors, see section 35(3).

[155] See *Boyle and Birds' Company Law* (3rd edn, Jordans, 1995), p. 99.

[156] E.g. a petition for unfair prejudice under section 459.

[157] See section 35A(4).

bring proceedings. Section 35A(1) provides that, in favour of a person dealing with a company in good faith, 'the power of the board of directors to bind the company, or authorise others to do so, shall be deemed to be free of any limitation under the company's constitution'. Under section 35A(4), this does not affect any right of a member of the company to bring proceedings to *restrain* the doing of an act which is beyond the powers of the company. Once again, this preserves a direct action to restrain 'unconstitutional' and unauthorised transactions by seeking an injunction. But 'no such proceedings shall lie in respect of an act done in fulfilment of a legal obligation arising from a previous act of the company'. Even before this reform in the law, the scope for minority shareholders to restrain the board (or individual directors) acting beyond its authority was in practice very limited. This was because of the wide power of management usually delegated to them by the articles.[158] It is the agency principles governing the authority of particular directors and officers that will normally determine the matter. However, the extended meaning given to 'limitations on directors' powers under the constitution' by section 35A(3) gives genuine protection to minority shareholders in private companies. It is extended to limitations deriving (a) from a resolution of the company in general meeting or a meeting of any class of shareholders or (b) from any agreement between the members of the company or of any class of shareholders. The provision in (a) above will reinforce the wider class rights[159] of shareholders where these are impinged on by transactions contemplated by the board.

A whole area of shareholder protection in private companies stems from shareholders' agreements with the company and the contractual remedies they afford. The provision in (b) above reinforces the protection given to such shareholders as a body or any class of them.[160] Such agreements may be made between the company and the members collateral to and supplementary to the articles. Alternatively, there may be agreement simply between all of the shareholders *inter se* or between only some of them (e.g. a class). Where shareholders are in a position to create appropriate agreements they can do much to strengthen their position. Shareholder agreements are not affected by the rule in *Foss* v. *Harbottle*. Any breach is therefore in principle actionable. The distinction between 'personal rights' and 'mere breaches' does not apply. The normal contractual remedy of damages for breach of contract is available and, in the appropriate conditions for such relief, an injunction might be obtained.

---

[158] See e.g. Article 72 of Table A.
[159] These rights are further discussed at p. 56 below.
[160] See further *Farrar's Company Law* (3rd ed., Butterworths, 1991), pp. 139–42.

A substantial difference to the existing law will be made by the proposals contained in the DTI's company law reform programme (*Modern Company Law for a Competitive Economy*).[161] This seeks a fundamental recasting of what is now section 14 of the Companies Act 1985. It proposes that, rather than deeming the constitution to be a contract of an unusual kind, the Act itself should set out the extent to which it gives rise to rights and obligations binding upon the company and enforceable by the company's members. Thus it will confer personal rights which are unaffected by ratification. The Act would also set out the remedies available for their enforcement. The statutory rights would be conferred on members as such and not on outsiders. The Act would set out a non-exhaustive list of personal rights. Those rights would reflect the personal rights already enjoyed (e.g. voting and participating in meetings). It would be left to the court to spell out any further rights that might be judicially deduced from the following phraseology: 'and any other right breach of which gives rise to direct harm to the member and not indirect or collective harm suffered as a result of damage done to the company as a whole'.[162] The Act would make it clear that the court could dismiss an action which is trivial or where the recognition of the personal right would not have made a material difference.

Due process and abuse of powers Another heterogeneous group of minority shareholders' direct claims relates neither to shareholders' personal rights nor to enforcing the provisions of the memorandum or articles of association. Instead, they relate to two broad areas of principle. Those are, first, fairness and due process in altering the constitution or passing resolutions in accordance with it. The second area consists of powers conferred by the articles on the board or general meeting (e.g. to allot further securities) which are improperly used to alter the balance of control so as to deprive the true majority of their voting control.

The most notable example of the principle of constitutional propriety or due process are the cases forming the traditional 'special majorities' exception to the rule in *Foss v. Harbottle*. Where there is any failure to comply with the requirements of a special or extraordinary resolution, any minority shareholder (not just one whose particular rights are

---

[161] See DTI Company Law Review Steering Group, *Modern Company Law for a Competitive Economy: Developing the Framework* (DTI, URN 00/656, March 2000), paras. 4.87–4.98. In DTI Company Law Review Steering Group, *Modern Company Law for a Competitive Economy: Final Report* (DTI, URN 01/942 and URN 01/943, July 2001), vol. I, para. 7.40, it is proposed that all constitutional rights should be enforced by individual members unless the contrary is provided in the constitution.

[162] See *ibid.*, question 4.4(d) and (e).

threatened) may complain.[163] This applies to high majority resolutions required by the Companies Act (e.g. to alter the articles) and extends to a provision in a particular company's articles requiring such a resolution even though this is not generally required. It may also be the case that a continuing course of conduct which defies a requirement in the articles may be regarded as an invalid *de facto* amendment rather than a mere breach.[164]

Another body of cases commonly known as the 'tricky notice' cases illustrate a lack of due process in operating the corporate constitution. Any notice of a special (or indeed any company resolution) must give a fair and reasonably full statement of the facts if the resolution is to bind the minority.[165] Where a misleading notice of a meeting is given, the resolution is invalid and a minority shareholder may bring proceedings.

The power of the majority to alter the articles by special resolution under section 9 of the Companies Act 1985 has long been held to be restrained by the obligations to act *bona fide* in the interests of the company as a whole. Although a number of aspects of this principle of equitable relief are controversial or lack clarity, it is clear that it provides some restraint from abuse of the majority's power to alter the articles by special resolution. Where shares are to be expropriated, adequate compensation must clearly be paid. There must be some advantage accruing to the company which shows the majority as reasonable when acting in good faith.[166] Except for one rather aberrant first instance decision,[167] this equitable principle is confined to special resolutions altering the articles as opposed to ordinary resolutions which impinge on shareholders' interests. Where the class rights of a shareholder can be varied or abrogated, special protection is afforded by statute[168] requiring the consent of the class in question.[169] In modern company law, it is increasingly likely that questions of class rights or *mala fide* alterations of the articles will be

---

[163] *Bailie* v. *Oriental Telephone Co.* [1915] 1 Ch 503 at 515 (CA); *Cotter* v. *National Union of Seamen* [1929] 2 Ch 58 at 69–70; *Edwards* v. *Halliwell* [1950] 2 All ER 104 at 106–7 (CA).

[164] This is one explanation of *Quin & Axtens* v. *Salmon* [1909] AC 442 (HL).

[165] *Kaye* v. *Croydon Tramways* [1898] 1 Ch 358 (CA); *Tiessen* v. *Henderson* [1899] 1 Ch 867; *MacConnell* v. *Prill* [1916] 2 Ch 57.

[166] For a detailed exploration of the case law, see *Boyle and Birds' Company Law* (4th edn, Jordans, 2000), paras. 4.27–4.30; and P. L. Davies (ed.), *Gower's Principles of Modern Company Law* (6th edn, London, Sweet & Maxwell, 1997), pp. 709–17.

[167] *Clements* v. *Clements Ltd* [1976] 2 All ER 208.

[168] Under sections 125–127 of the Companies Act 1985.

[169] There may be problems in establishing whether a class right is affected and what is meant by abrogation or variation. See *Boyle and Birds' Company Law* (4th edn, Jordans, 2000), paras. 8.7.1–8.7.2; and P. L. Davies (ed.), *Gower's Principles of Modern Company Law* (6th ed., London, Sweet & Maxwell, 1997), pp. 717–26.

litigated by an unfair prejudice petition under section 459 rather than under the more traditional procedures.[170]

A somewhat controversial source of minority shareholders' direct claims against the company (in which the directors may also be joined) may in some situations be based on fiduciary duty. This occurs where the directors have abused their powers under the articles in a way which directly impacts on the minority's shares. This is unquestionably the case where the board exercises a standard form power in the articles of a private company to refuse a transfer of their shares. Here the long-established case law gives shareholders a right of action where the board have acted in bad faith or for a collateral purpose.[171]

The directors' duties of good faith and proper purpose have long been applied also to the board's power to allot share capital. Here likewise it can be argued that a direct shareholder's claim may lie against the company.[172] On this analysis, the true basis of an action grounded on improper purpose in issuing shares is 'an alleged infringement of the petitioner's individual rights as shareholder'.[173] Other English authorities are less clear. These cases make it clear that an allotment of shares for an improper purpose, even though bad faith cannot be shown, may be challenged. Where the lawful majority have been deprived of their existing control by a *coup d'état* achieved through the board's power to allot, such an allotment will simply be invalidated at the instance of the true majority.[174] The analysis required is more subtle where it is a minority shareholder who purports to act on behalf of 'the majority'. Here the minority are asserting the rights of the majority as a matter of 'due process' on constitutional property. In *Hogg* v. *Cramphorn*,[175] Buckley J made it clear that this was why the question of the propriety of the allotment had to be submitted to a shareholders' meeting at which the disputed shares would not be voted. The minority shareholder complained of a wrong neither to himself nor primarily to the company. It was, as Buckley J pointed out, an attempt 'to deprive the majority of their constitutional rights', which attempt would 'cease to have any

---

[170] See Chapter 4 below.

[171] See *Boyle and Birds' Company Law* (4th edn, Jordans, 2000), para. 9.2.1. In some situations, directors owe a fiduciary duty directly to shareholders (rather than the company, as is overwhelmingly the general rule): see *Gething* v. *Kilner* [1972] 2 WLR 337.

[172] See *Re A Company* [1986] BCLC 82. See further *Southern Treatment Co. Ltd* v. *Southern Resources Ltd (No. 4)* (1988) 14 ACLR 569 (Supreme Court of Southern Australia).

[173] *Re A Company* [1986] BCLC 82 at 84 *per* Hoffmann J. This was a section 459 petition.

[174] *Punt* v. *Symons* [1903] 2 Ch 506; *Piercy* v. *Mills* [1920] 1 Ch 77. In both cases, the 'majority and the minority were already arranged for battle on a specific issue when the latter attempted to create reinforcements by issuing additional shares': *Hogg* v. *Cramphorn Ltd* [1967] 2 Ch 254 at 269 *per* Buckley J.

[175] [1967] 2 Ch 254.

force' if (leaving aside the wrongly issued shares) the majority in fact approved of what had been done.[176] If a majority are allowed to vindicate the rights of the majority, it is obvious that if the majority, when alerted to this, nevertheless agreed to what has been done, then *cadit quaestio*.

The procedural form of shareholders' claims

The long-established case law shows plainly that it is a matter of choice for the minority plaintiff whether the action is brought in his or her name as the party (or parties if there are several) of record or as a non-derivative representative action on behalf of the shareholders as a whole or a class or group of them. Either type of shareholders' direct claim can be found in the law reports for enforcing direct claims.[177]

The reform of civil procedure expressed in the Civil Procedure Rules 2000 has not restricted this freedom of choice. Until quite recently Order 15, rule 12 was kept in force by the Civil Procedure Rules 1998.[178] The Civil Procedure Rules 2000,[179] Part 19, rule 19.6 now governs 'representative parties with the same interest'. The simple and clear language of rule 19.6 appears to create no problems for shareholders seeking to bring a direct claim in representative form. It seems likely that the existing case law on such shareholders' representative proceedings will still be applicable. Thus the 'clean hands' doctrine will apply to the conduct of the plaintiff.[180] The plaintiff in a representative claim has the right to control the proceedings until judgment unless the court otherwise directs.[181]

In a shareholder's claim against the company it is not necessary to join the directors as parties, unless some form of relief is sought against them in addition to the remedy against the company. However, in such an action it is possible to seek relief by way of injunction against the company while joining the directors as co-defendants in order that relief is claimed against them for the company's benefit.[182] In such a claim the two forms

---

[176] [1967] Ch 254 at 269. In *Bamford* v. *Bamford* [1970] Ch 212 (CA), this passage from Buckley J's judgment was cited with approval. In *Howard Smith Ltd* v. *Ampol Petroleum Ltd* [1974] AC 821 (PC) the proceedings were brought by the 'true majority'.

[177] E.g. *Pender* v. *Lushington* (1877) 6 ChD 70; *Mosely* v. *Koffyfontein Mines Ltd* [1911] 1 Ch 73 (representative proceedings); *Simpson* v. *Westminster Palace Hotel* (1860) 8 HLC 712; and *Sidebottom* v. *Kersham Leese & Co. Ltd* [1921] 1 Ch 154 (CA) (personal action).

[178] SI 1998 No. 3132. See Schedule 1.   [179] SI 2000 No. 221, Schedule 2.

[180] *Burt* v. *British Nation Life Insurance Association* (1859) 4 De G & J 158. But cf *Moseley* v. *Koffyfontein Mines* [1911] 1 Ch 73 (CA), an action to restrain future illegal acts. An application can be made under rule 19.6(2) to replace a person acting as representative.

[181] Rule 19.6(4).

[182] See *Russell* v. *Wakefield Waterworks* (1875) LR 20 Eq 474 at 481–2; *Hogg* v. *Cramphorn Ltd* [1967] 2 Ch 254.

of relief should arise out of a series of related transactions. The court will not allow what is in substance a derivative suit to be brought in the guise of a representative action in tort (e.g. the tort of conspiracy).[183]

Financing 'direct' claims

It is well established that a costs indemnity order, commonly known as a *Wallersteiner* order,[184] cannot be made in a shareholders' claim which is not a derivative one.[185] However, at the end of the proceedings an order may be made on a 'common fund' basis if the result of the case is beneficial to the members generally.[186] The 'revolution' in funding litigation, introduced by section 58 of the Courts and Legal Services Act 1990 and implemented by subsequent delegated legislation,[187] may allow the use of conditional fee agreements in any civil proceedings the object of which is the recovery of a money judgment. In most types of 'direct claim', it has been seen that the remedy sought is an injunction or declaration. Such proceedings are obviously beyond the scope of the legislation. However, where the shareholder seeks capital payments or unpaid dividends, conditional fee agreements are available. A breach of a shareholders' agreement may give a claim in damages for breach of contract which would likewise render such claims amenable. Remedies in respect of allotments of shares made on the basis of false or misleading statements would also be included.[188]

---

[183] *Burland* v. *Earle* [1902] AC 83 at 93 (PC); *Prudential Assurance Co. Ltd* v. *Newman Industries Ltd (No. 2)* [1982] Ch 204; *Heron International* v. *Lord Grade* [1983] BCLC 244 at 281–3.

[184] See *Wallersteiner* v. *Moir (No. 2)* [1975] QB 373.

[185] *Marx* v. *Estates and General Ltd* [1976] 1 WLR 380 at 392. See also *Re A Company* [1986] BCLC 82.

[186] *Marx* v. *Estates and General Ltd* [1976] 1 WLR 380.

[187] See the Conditional Fee Agreements Order 1998 (SI 1998 No. 1860) which allows the use of such agreements in all civil proceedings within the scope of section 58 of the Courts and Legal Services Act 1990.

[188] See section 111A of the Companies Act 1985 (as amended) which allows claims for damages against the company in respect of such allotments. See also cases like *Gething* v. *Kilner* [1972] 1 WLR 337.

3   A new derivative action

Introduction

In 1997, the Law Commission completed its task of reviewing and re-forming the law on shareholders' remedies. The Law Commission published its Consultation Paper on shareholders' remedies in 1996[1] and its Report in October 1997.[2] The central feature of the Law Commission's proposals is a 'new derivative action'. This important proposed change in the law on minority shareholders' remedies is worth detailed attention. The Report contains both draft legislation in the form of a 'Draft Companies (Members Proceedings) Bill'[3] with the all-important detailed procedure fleshed out in the 'Draft Civil Procedure Rules on Derivative Claims'.[4] The Department of Trade and Industry later published its own Consultation Paper on shareholder remedies.[5] This indicates unqualified approval of the Law Commission's proposal for a statutory derivative action in English law.[6] It is therefore not unreasonable to draw the conclusion that, it is hoped before not too long, Parliament may enact the Law Commission's new derivative remedy. Certainly, this would be possible without awaiting further structural reforms of company law.

---

[1] Law Commission, *Shareholder Remedies: A Consultation Paper* (Law Commission Consultation Paper No. 142, Stationery Office, 1996).

[2] Law Commission, *Shareholder Remedies* (Law Commission Report No. 246, Cm 3769, Stationery Office, 1997).

[3] See *ibid.*, Appendix A. This should become section 455A of the Companies Act 1985.

[4] See *ibid.*, Appendix B. This will become Draft Part 56 of the Civil Procedure Rules 1998.

[5] DTI, URN 98/994, November 1998.

[6] The DTI does, however, raise questions about the jurisdictional arrangements for the equivalent proposal for a new derivative action in Scotland. See Law Commission, *Shareholder Remedies* (Law Commission Report No. 246, Cm 3769, Stationery Office, 1997), Appendix A; and DTI Consultation Paper, paras. 3.13–3.15. Questions are also raised about the Law Commission's proposals in respect of the unfair prejudice remedy. See footnote 187 below as to the Consultation Papers from the Company Law Review Steering Group.

In both its Consultation Paper and in its Report on shareholder remedies, the Law Commission accepts the failure of the old existing 'common law' derivative action.[7] The Commission accepts the general 'philosophical' approach of the rule in *Foss* v. *Harbottle* in terms of general principles. 'Our view was that the basic approach to the right to bring a derivative action was a sound one: an individual shareholder should only be able to bring such an action in exceptional circumstances.'[8]

The Report adopts[9] the classical statement of the rule itself and the exceptions to it in *Edwards* v. *Halliwell*[10] as restated in *Prudential Assurance Co. Ltd* v. *Newman Industries Ltd (No. 2)*.[11] Indeed, in the introduction to the Report,[12] the Commission sets forth six 'guiding principles' for reform of shareholders' remedies. As the Report indicates in Part 6, some of these principles clearly reflect the traditional approach embodied in the *Foss* v. *Harbottle* rule.[13]

It will be seen that the Law Commission has adopted what became a well-established model adopted widely in Commonwealth countries.[14] Essentially, this statutory replacement for the common law derivative action requires the minority shareholder to obtain the leave of the court before bringing a derivative action to enforce breaches of directors' duties. The Report stresses that the new statutory procedure should 'be subject to tight judicial control at all stages'.[15] Indeed, it will be seen that the judicial discretion as to the grant of leave is more hedged about by restricting guidelines than in some of the earlier Commonwealth legislation.[16] It is somewhat surprising that the comparative law research embodied in the Consultation Paper (and relied upon the Report) is confined in scope to those developments in Commonwealth legislation. Apart from a brief footnote reference to the Fifth Company Law Directive,[17] there is no exploration of the relevant law of even the leading Member States of the European Union. Even if the Fifth Company Law Directive and the European Company project continue to gather dust, it would seem desirable that the minority shareholder remedies in such significant EU states

---

[7] Consultation Paper, para. 10.1; Report, paras. 6.1–6.7.

[8] Report, para. 6.4.   [9] Report, para. 6.2.

[10] [1950] 2 All ER 1064 at 1066–9 *per* Jenkins LJ.

[11] [1982] Ch 204 (CA).   [12] See Report, para. 1.10.

[13] See the 'Guiding Principles' (i) on the proper plaintiff; (ii) on internal management; and (vi) on freedom from unnecessary shareholder interference.

[14] See Report, para. 6.8, Consultation Paper, paras. 16.8 and 16.23.

[15] Report, para. 6.6.

[16] See the Canadian Business Corporations Act 1974–75–76, section 239; and the Ghana Companies Code 1963, section 10. See Consultation Paper, Appendix B.

[17] See Report, para. 6.9, footnote 23.

as France and Germany should be given some minimal attention – even if only to discuss their relevance!

It is also surprising that the American derivative action is almost totally ignored.[18] In the common law world, the creation of an effective and actively used shareholders' derivative action is very largely an American achievement. The Consultation Paper[19] contains no discussion of the American background either in the explorations of the existing law in Section B or in framing the new derivative action in Part 16 (in Section E). The same is true of the Report. It is difficult to imagine that American law would be so completely ignored if a major area of, say, the law of contract or tort were being considered for reform by the Law Commission. This is not to deny that the various models supplied by Canadian and other Commonwealth legislation are the most appropriate basis for reform. What is strange is that there is no attempt at comparative treatment of either American or European law even if only to demonstrate the superiority of the Commonwealth models.

The 'scope' of the new remedy

Under the heading 'availability of the new derivative action', the Report considers what wrongs to the company may be the subject of a derivative action. Essentially, the answer is that the new remedy is confined to dealing with the consequences of breaches of duty to the company by its directors.[20] The Report contains a more refined analysis than the Consultation Paper and reaches different conclusions on some important points of policy. As with the 'common law' derivative action, the new procedure may not be used to bring corporate claims against third parties (e.g. for breach of contract or the commission of a tort) which exist independently of any breach of directors' duties.[21] It may be possible, however, to pursue a derivative claim based on a breach of directors' duties against a third party. This will be justified where general equitable principles permit remedies against such parties (e.g. under the rules for constructive trusts or tracing).[22] The Report concedes that the directors, by failing to pursue an action (say in contract or tort) against a third party,

[18] For the historical origins of the derivative action in Anglo-American law, see Chapters 1 and 2 above.

[19] In the Consultation Paper, Appendix G includes a brief extract from the American Federal Rules of Civil Procedure, but is otherwise confined to Commonwealth legislation.

[20] Report, paras. 6.23–6.57; Consultation Paper, paras. 16.9–16.11.

[21] Report, paras. 6.32–6.34. See also Report, Appendix A (Draft Bill), section 458A(2).

[22] See Report, Appendix A (Draft Bill), section 458(3).

may themselves be in breach of duty for failing to do so (e.g. for breach of their duty of skill and care).[23]

Majority shareholders

In defining the scope of the new derivative action in terms of breaches of directors' duties, the Report[24] considers situations where there is no breach of duty by the directors. Here the concern is that a group of majority or controlling shareholders may be sued. The problem is that under the 'common law' derivative action such shareholders can be pursued where the criteria for 'fraud on a minority' are satisfied. The Law Commission came to a firm policy decision that such a claim will not be possible under the new statutory action.[25] The Report first examined Megarry VC's decision in *Estmanco (Kilner House) Ltd* v. *Greater London Council*[26] as an illustration of a derivative action against a wrongdoing majority shareholder.[27] The Report concludes that in such cases 'what is in issue is a shareholder's personal rights against the company because of the conduct of the majority; it is not the company's rights against which are being infringed. The appropriate remedy for the shareholder is a personal action under the articles of association or (more likely) a claim under section 459 of the Companies Act 1985, rather than a derivative action on behalf of the company.'[28] This enables the Law Commission to keep the new remedy within the narrow compass of a 'breach of duty by director', but as a policy decision it is open to question.

Where a dominant majority of shareholders (or indeed a coherent minority able to exercise *de facto* control over the board) causes harm to the company, derivative proceedings may well be the most appropriate remedy against them (especially in the case of a listed plc) where the majority, overbearing an honest board of directors, have fraudulently hived-off assets to their personal benefit (possibly in the immediate aftermath of a takeover bid). Here then the most appropriate remedy would appear to be restitution to the company for the benefit of all shareholders.[29]

Somewhat strangely, the Report makes no cross-reference to its own definition of 'directors' for the purpose of the new remedy. However, it

[23] Report, para. 6.34 and Report, Appendix A (Draft Bill), section 458A(2)(a).
[24] Report, para. 6.27.   [25] Report, paras. 6.28–6.30.
[26] [1982] 1 WLR 2. See Report, paras. 6.28–6.29.
[27] I.e. the Greater London Council, who had compelled the board of directors to withdraw the company's action against them.
[28] Report, para. 6.30.
[29] See, for example, the *locus classicus* of derivative proceedings, *Menier* v. *Hoopers Telegraph Works* (1874) 9 Ch App 350.

later appears[30] that 'directors' is to include both *de facto* and 'shadow directors'. This latter term[31] may sometimes enable majority shareholders (at least in a private company) to be brought within the scope of the new remedy. However, a more flexible concept of 'corporate controller' might with advantage have been defined to meet the situations that may arise, even if only infrequently, in public listed companies.

In the various Commonwealth models of statutory derivative action which were considered in both the Consultation Paper and the Report,[32] it is not the general pattern to confine the remedy to breaches of directors' duties.[33] It would seem that the Law Commission has preferred conceptual clarity to a more flexible approach to the protection of the genuine needs of the company and its shareholders.

Officers and employees

The other major category of 'non-director' excluded from the new remedy is that of 'officers and employees'.[34] The Consultation Paper[35] left open the possibility of using the new remedy against managers and officers who were not directors, but placed it on a more restrictive basis than in the case of proceedings against directors. For this purpose the Consultation Paper reintroduced what was essentially the old concept of 'fraud on a minority' (as found in common law derivative actions). 'We anticipate that it would only be in very rare circumstances that advantage would have to be taken of this provision, since in most situations there would also be a breach of duty by the directors.'[36] This limited preservation of the common law concept was plainly unsatisfactory. This was especially the case in so far as the concept of 'wrongdoer control' as applied in the context of a public listed company was concerned.[37]

The Report has wisely rejected this dual approach, but has adopted the questionable solution of excluding managers and officers from the new

---

[30] See Report, para. 6.36.
[31] See Companies Act 1989, section 741(2): 'In relation to a company "shadow director" means a person in accordance with whose directions or instructions the directors of the company are accustomed to act.' See *Gore-Browne on Companies* (Jordans, looseleaf), para. 27.2.
[32] See Consultation Paper, Appendices F and G; and Report, para. 6.8.
[33] See the Australian Second Corporate Law Simplification Bill, section 245A(1); the Canadian Business Corporation Act 1974–75–76, section 239; and the New Zealand Companies Act 1993, section 165. Compare the Republic of South Africa Companies Act No. 61 of 1973, section 266; and the Ghana Companies Code 1963, section 210.
[34] See Report, paras. 6.42–6.46.   [35] See Report, paras. 16.10–16.11.
[36] Consultation Paper, para. 16.11.
[37] The reference to 'the fifth limb' of the rule in *Foss* v. *Harbottle* as restated in *Prudential Assurance Co. Ltd* v. *Newman Industries Ltd (No. 2)* 1982 Ch 204 makes this clear.

remedy.[38] The Report's reasoning for confining the remedy to directors is as follows:

> The decision on what action to take against employees is very clearly a manage-ment decision for the board of directors. Where the claim is not against a director (or arising out of a breach of duty by directors) the board should be making an unbiased decision on the merits of suing and will probably be much better placed than an individual shareholder to evaluate the costs and benefits involved.

As further 'make weights', the Report adds (in addition to the potential for interference with what are management decisions) the potential for vexatious litigation by disgruntled shareholders against employees. This 'may well be unfair to the employees concerned'. In the case of public companies, the Report asserts, 'there is a risk that shares will be acquired for the sole purpose of bringing proceedings where the person acquiring the share is unhappy with particular management decisions'.[39] These illustrations of possible abuses could readily be dealt with by the exercise of the court's powers to grant leave. It will be seen later[40] that the court has ample powers in deciding whether or not to grant leave to block abusive applications.[41]

The Report concludes that by 'focusing on breaches of duty by direc-tors the derivative action will be placed on a more logical and rational basis'. This, however, ignores a number of practical difficulties. It is of course clear that the Law Commission's solution would allow not only the board of directors as a whole (or a majority of the board) to be tar-geted as defendants, but would also allow individual board members to be proceeded against. Thus a managing director or other executive direc-tor who acted in breach of duty without the board's knowledge or assent could be singled out as defendant in a derivative action.[42] Nevertheless, the assumption that a senior officer or executive not on the board (e.g. a general manager or finance officer) may grossly breach his or her fidu-ciary duty to the company without fear of being the subject of minority shareholder proceedings is very much open to question. The board of directors may fail to act for unsatisfactory or inexplicable reasons. Great harm may nevertheless have been done to the company.

It is true that the Report elsewhere proposes that the new remedy may be brought for breach of the directors' duties of care and skill.[43] However, the Report's proposals (in the context of application for leave to bring the

---

[38] Report, paras. 6.42–6.46.   [39] Report, para. 16.45.   [40] See p. 74 below.
[41] For example, one of the 'guidelines' is concerned with the applicant's good faith and another with the 'interests of the company'. See Report, paras. 6.75–6.79.
[42] See draft section 458A(2) in Appendix A to the Report.
[43] See Report, paras. 6.38–6.64. See p. 67 below.

new remedy) in respect of shareholder ratification and shareholder powers to decree that no action should be brought to remedy a wrong to the company, make it unlikely that such an action for negligence by the board would succeed. Especially in the case of public listed companies with widely scattered shareholdings (where the board is in *de facto* control), it is important that serious fraud or misappropriation of assets by officers and managers below board level should not be immune from minority shareholder litigation. The board may have their own motives for suppressing litigation. Dismissal of dishonest officers or senior managers should not be allowed to become the only possible remedy.

In the case of groups of companies, it is even more unsatisfactory to confine the derivative action to members of the board of the parent holding company. The Report's rejection[44] of multiple derivative actions adds to the dimension of this problem. The need to expose fraud and serious abuse in groups of companies would seem to require a more realistic approach.

The full range of directors' duties

While limiting the scope of the statutory derivative action to breaches of directors' duties, the Report[45] (like the Consultation Paper)[46] makes clear that it is potentially available as a means of enforcing the whole range of directors' duties. It will be seen that this includes statutory fiduciary duties and the duty of skill and care.

The Report deals with a pedantic if scholarly point raised by some consultees that, if *Movitex Ltd* v. *Bulfield*[47] correctly states the law, the conflict of duty and interest rule is a rule of disability and not a fiduciary duty. The Report, while accepting that Movitex does draw very difficult distinctions, does not attempt to resolve the issue in terms of the correct analysis of the obligation of a director not to place himself or herself in a position where his or her personal interests conflict with those of the company. As with other issues on the substantive law of directors' duties, the Law Commission regards such issues as beyond the remit of its review of shareholder remedies.[48] Instead, the Report proposes that 'the legislation should make it clear that a derivative action is available where a cause of action arises as a result of a director putting himself in a position where his personal interests conflict with his duties to the company'.[49]

---

[44] See Report, para. 6.109, discussed at p. 85 below.   [45] Report, para. 6.49.
[46] Consultation Paper, paras. 16.8–16.10.   [47] [1988] BCLC 104.
[48] Report, paras. 6.26 and 6.48.
[49] Report, para. 6.48; and see Report, Appendix A (draft) section 458A(2)(b).

One respondent (to the Consultation Paper) raised the argument that it was fallacious to say that directors were under a 'duty' to use their powers for a proper purpose. The Report tersely concludes that the Law Commission is not convinced by this argument.[50]

The Report emphasises that the term 'breach of duty' shall comprise, *inter alia*, a statutory default by a director. It is made clear that this will include the statutory fiduciary duties laid down in Part X of the Companies Act 1985.[51] It has been a moot point whether the common law derivative action would allow a minority shareholder to enforce these duties. It can be contended that civil remedies provided for would to a considerable extent be rendered redundant without such a possibility.[52]

One of the most potentially significant proposals in the Report is that it firmly asserts that the new procedure should be made available for breach of directors' duties of care and skill.[53] The Report brushes aside various arguments by a minority of consultees who opposed this advance on the common law derivative action. Reference was made to the risk of increased litigation by disgruntled shareholders, to the assumption of misguided managerial decisions and mistakes inherent in the decision to invest, and to the danger of discouraging people from becoming directors. The Report deals firmly with such arguments. It cites one consultee who rightly contends that well-organised and competent companies run by directors who know and follow their respective duties have nothing to fear.[54] As for the argument of increased litigation, this is dismissed as 'overstated'. The Report stresses that, under its proposals for the court's discretion as to grant of leave, there will be tight judicial control. The Report rightly observes that there is no reason why directors should shelter behind a procedural rule[55] to escape liability. However, it will be seen that, since the directors' duty of care and skill is one the breach of which may be ratified, the court's discretion to grant leave may prove much more difficult to obtain than in the cases of breaches of duty not open to ratification. It may also be observed that the Law Commission's Final Report[56] on the duties of company directors firmly proposes raising the standard of skill and care required of directors.[57]

---

[50] Report, paras. 6.25–6.26, citing *Rolled Steel Products (Holdings) Ltd* v. *British Steel Corp.* [1984] BCLC 466. See also *Howard Smith Ltd* v. *Ampol Petroleum Ltd* [1974] AC 821 (PC).

[51] The Report refers to failure to obtain approval for a substantial property transaction involving a director under section 320. See Report, para. 6.47, footnote 69.

[52] See *Gore-Browne on Companies*, para. 28.7.

[53] Report, paras. 6.38–6.41. Consultation Paper, para. 16.9.   [54] Report, para. 6.40.

[55] I.e. the traditional *Foss* v. *Harbottle* rule.

[56] Law Commission, *Company Directors: Regulating Conflicts of Interest and Formulating a Statement of Duties* (Law Commission Report No. 261, 1999).

[57] See ibid., Part 5 at para. 5.20.

The abolition of the common law derivative action

The Report[58] notes that the vast majority of respondents agreed with the provisional view in the Consultation Paper[59] that the common law derivative action should no longer be available once the new statutory derivative action is in force. Thus the new procedure will replace entirely the common law right to bring a derivative action. Although this question was resolved differently in the Canadian legislation, in more recent Commonwealth legislation the common law remedy is simply replaced by the new remedy.[60]

The Report notes that the common law derivative action must be used where damages or property are being recovered for the company by a minority shareholder on the ground of *ultra vires* or illegality. Where a 'personal action' on these grounds is brought the derivative form is not appropriate. This is so because in a personal action the plaintiff minority shareholder seeks only an injunction or declaration to prohibit the company acting in an *ultra vires* or illegal way. In derivative proceedings on the grounds of *ultra vires* or illegality the crucial difference is that, in consequence of a transaction being set aside, property or damages are being recovered for the company. The Report[61] indicates that the same distinction now applies to shareholders' actions under the special majorities exception to the *Foss* v. *Harbottle* rule. In all these cases, the Report proposes to bring such derivative actions within the ambit of the new statutory procedure by 'regarding' the defendant directors as having acted in breach of duty for the purpose of the new procedure.[62] Thus the new derivative procedure should replace the common law derivative action entirely.[63]

Personal actions

In the case of what the Report[64] terms the existing personal actions, the common law procedure will continue to operate on the ground that such personal actions 'fall outside' the rule in *Foss* v. *Harbottle* since it 'does not apply to them'. Thus a shareholder's 'personal action' for individual rights derived from the articles, or on the 'special majorities' ground, or challenging a proposed illegal or *ultra vires* act, will not be governed by the new procedure.[65] An application for leave of the court or any

---

[58] Report, para. 6.51.   [59] Consultation Paper, para. 16.13.
[60] Report, para. 6.52.   [61] Report, para. 6.54.   [62] Report.
[63] Report, para. 6.55.   [64] Report, paras. 6.56–6.57.
[65] Report, para. 6.57. As to common law 'direct actions', see further Chapter 2, p. 49 above. As to the reform of section 14 of the Companies Act 1985, see Chapter 2, p. 55 above.

other procedural requirement of the new derivative action will simply be inapplicable.[66]

While the general policy is both clear and satisfactory, there may be some confusion over the Report's treatment of 'derivative' and 'personal' actions. At common law this turns essentially on what remedy is being sought. Where an injunction or declaration is sought it is not strictly accurate to call such an action derivative even if the consequence is to benefit both the plaintiff minority shareholders and the defendant company. Moreover, the Report fails to distinguish the shareholders' representative action. Instead of using the slightly confusing term 'personal action' (which implies a shareholder is seeking to enforce 'personal rights'), it might be an aid to clarity to adopt the American term 'direct action' as the correlative of the 'derivative' action. This action applies to proceedings relating not only to the 'personal' or 'individual' rights of shareholders (under the articles or otherwise) but also to proceedings seeking relief by way of injunction or declaration on the basis of the special majorities exception as well as action seeking similar relief on the basis of illegal or *ultra vires* activity.[67] Even actions in respect of directors' duties (where monetary compensation or the restitution of corporate property is not involved) are more accurately described as 'direct' rather than 'derivative'. This would apply to an action seeking to prohibit a proposed transaction in breach of directors' duty of good faith or proper purpose. 'Direct' actions ('personal' actions is the Law Commission's preferred terminology) can at the plaintiff's option be either 'individual' actions where only the plaintiffs of record are involved, or ordinary representative actions on behalf of other shareholders where rights are similarly affected. Such shareholders' ordinary representative actions are not of course to be confused with 'common law' derivative actions.[68]

The Report, whether intentionally or not, appears to blur some of these distinctions. Thus there is no recognition in the Report's very brief account of 'personal action' of the existence of shareholders' representative actions which are not derivative. The draft section 458A(1)[69] gives a definition of the new derivative action as 'an action by a member of a company where the cause of action is vested in the company and relief is sought on its behalf'. Where the sole relief being sought is an injunction or declaration this will make the line between 'derivative' and 'personal' proceedings hard to discern. Since, for example, minority shareholders' actions based on *ultra vires* or illegal action may be 'deemed' derivative[70]

---

[66] Report, para. 6.56.

[67] The Report recognises that all such proceedings are 'personal actions'; see Report, para. 6.57.

[68] See *Gore-Browne on Companies*, para. 28.10.   [69] Report, Appendix A.

[70] Report, para. 6.54.

where a director causes the company to act in those ways, if an injunction is the only remedy sought, is the proceeding a derivative one within the terms of section 458A(1) and (2) or do the old 'common law' distinctions still prevail? The somewhat terse observations in the Report give no clear answer.

The plaintiff in derivative actions

In the common law derivative action, former shareholders (including those who were members at the time a wrong was done to the company) may not bring derivative proceedings. Current members (even if they were not members at the time the corporate cause of action arose) are the only plaintiffs entitled to bring such proceedings. The Report confirms that this will remain the position since it accurately reflects the nature of the derivative action.[71]

Primary legislation and rules of court: implementation of the new procedure

An important innovation in the Report[72] is to set out the nature of the new remedy in a proposed new section 458A[73] in the Companies Act 1985, but to limit this primary legislation to the basic essentials of the new remedy. The detailed procedure for the application for leave to bring a derivative action is spelt out in the draft rules of court.[74] This approach will clearly have the advantage that it will shield the details of the proposed procedure from adverse (or destructive) attack when the primary legislative provision is examined in Parliament. It may also allow judges to be more flexible in interpreting the new rules of court than if they had to deal with primary legislation.

The Report justifies the need for the essentials of the new remedy to be embodied in primary legislation for two reasons. First, the Scottish Law Commission has insisted that a new derivative action in Scotland must be fully set out in primary legislation.[75]

Secondly, the Law Commission considers that it is desirable to include a concise provision as to the English derivative remedy in the Companies Act so that it will alert shareholders to its existence and put it on the same

---

[71] Report, para. 6.50.

[72] Report, paras. 6.16–6.21. See, however, the Consultation Paper's consideration of 'Case Management by the Courts of Shareholder Proceedings' (Part 17).

[73] See Report, Appendix A.   [74] See Report, Appendix B.

[75] See Report, paras. 6.17, 6.22 and Appendix D. The Scots law proposals are considered below.

basis as the statutory unfair prejudice remedy.[76] The Report intends that the 'Draft Rule in Derivative Claims' (set out in Appendix B) should be adopted by the Civil Rule Procedure Committee.[77] The draft rule is intended to tie in with the then Draft Proceedings Rules as closely as possible: 'We have endeavoured to adopt the vocabulary and approach of the latter in forming our own rule. However, the rules are still being prepared. It may be necessary, therefore, for some minor adjustments to be made to the draft rule on derivative actions to incorporate it into the general body of rules in due course.'[78]

The procedural framework for the application of leave

Notice to the company Before seeking the leave of the court to proceed in the new derivative action, the plaintiff must as a precondition give notice, which in most cases must be twenty-eight days. This requirement can be waived if the shareholder can show that urgent relief is required and/or if the court dispenses with the requirement of notice. The notice must specify the grounds of the proposed derivative action.[79] The notice requirement (common in existing Commonwealth legislation on derivative actions) is an obvious necessity to allow the board of directors either to take its own remedial action or to prepare a proper response to the plaintiff shareholders' application.

When the application for leave is heard The Report, before turning to the factors that should influence the exercise of the court's discretion to grant leave, seeks to provide a procedural framework for that process. The Law Commission's view is that the 'convenient stage' for the court to consider the grant of leave might be at the close of proceedings but it should have a discretion to do so at an earlier stage if it thought fit.[80] The application would normally be heard by a judge rather than a master. All the parties to the proceedings should be parties to the application for leave. As such, they should be entitled to receive evidence filed in the application and to be present unless the court otherwise directs.

The Report confirms the provisional view in the Consultation Paper that, where there is to be a case management conference, it will normally be convenient for the issue of leave to be dealt with at that stage.

[76] Report, para. 6.18.   [77] Under section 1(2) of the Civil Procedure Act 1997.
[78] Report, para. 6.21. See further *ibid.*, paras. 1.28–1.30. As to the Civil Procedure Rules 1998 and 2000, see Chapter 2, pp. 32–6 above.
[79] Report, paras. 6.58–6.59; Consultation Paper, paras. 16.15–16.17.
[80] Consultation Paper, para. 16.18; Report, paras. 6.66–6.67.

The Report goes further to propose that it would be appropriate to require the court to fix a case management conference for all derivative
actions.[81] Normally, all parties to the proceedings will be present at
the case management conference.[82] In an appropriate case, it may also
be possible for a respondent to apply to strike out the claims at the
outset.[83]

On the application for leave the court is given the following powers: (a)
to grant leave to continue the claim for such period and on such terms
as the court thinks fit; (b) to refuse leave and dismiss the claim; (c) to
strike out the claim; and (d) to adjourn the proceedings relating to the
application and give such directions as it thinks fit.[84] The Report proposes
that, if the claimant does not apply for leave at the case management
conference (or at such earlier time as the court directs), the defendant
should be able to apply to strike out the claim.[85]

The issues relevant to the grant of leave

The Report,[86] following the Consultation Paper,[87] concluded that in considering the issue of leave the court should take into account all the relevant circumstances without limit. The Report,[88] however, also lists 'five
specific matters' which the court should take into account in exercising
its broad discretion. The Report[89] notes that the majority of respondents
agreed with the provisional view in the Consultation Paper[90] that the
court should consider all the circumstances without limit. The Report[91]
observes that it is important for the court to have the flexibility to look at
all the relevant circumstances. 'There is a danger that any definitive criteria for granting leave would be incomplete and would not fit the circumstances of individual cases.' A minority of respondents expressed concern
that this approach would mean that the reasons for deciding whether a
claim should proceed would be vague and that it would be difficult to
advise clients with any certainty as to what the result of an application
for leave would be. The Law Commission counters this by saying that
'concerns about difficulties in predicting the outcome of applications for
leave are overstated . . . we also propose a list of specific matters which
the court should take into account, and we consider that these, together

---

[81] Report, para. 6.67.
[82] The Report refers to the Lord Chancellor's Department Working Party on Judicial Case
Management, para. 4.8. See Draft Rules 50.5 and 50.6 in Appendix B.
[83] Report, para. 6.67; and Draft Rule 50.4(4) and (5).
[84] Report, para. 6.68; and Draft Rule 50.8(1).
[85] Report, para. 6.68; and Draft Rule 50.6(3).
[86] Report, para. 6.70.   [87] Consultation Paper, para. 16.25.   [88] Report, para. 6.74.
[89] Report, para. 6.72.   [90] Consultation Paper, para. 16.25.   [91] Report, para. 6.73.

with the developing case law, will assist practitioners in advising their clients'.[92]

The list of non-binding criteria may not, however, have the benign effect that the Law Commission intends. In the Consultation Paper, the Law Commission first lists a number of arguments against the approach it has adopted,[93] followed by counter-arguments in favour.[94] The four arguments against a broad flexible discretion are described in the Consultation Paper as follows:

The first is that a list may appear to be a set of hurdles which applicants have to overcome and which would deter them. Secondly, it could be seen as maintaining a policy of not favouring derivative actions and as a signal to adopt an over-restrictive approach to them. Thirdly, it could be seen as constraining the flexible exercise of discretion which we are anxious to encourage, in that inclusion of these and omission of others may suggest that these are the only relevant criteria or the most important. The fourth argument against such a list is that it is not truly helpful by way of guidance to advisers or shareholders in relation to 'good faith' and 'interests of the company' because they are open textured phrases which have been given numerous meanings by different courts.

The present writer finds these arguments much more impressive that the counter-arguments on which the Consultation Paper relies in formulating its wide discretion. In answering 'the criticism' of the 'four arguments', the Law Commission states that 'we intend that the wording should make plain that the discretion is wide and that matters set out are only some examples of the circumstances to which the courts should have regard'. As regards the problem of advisers and shareholders, the response is that 'although advisers will have to carry out further research, express reference to these factors will be of some assistance'.[95] The Consultation Paper then concludes:

The most important advantage of listing them is that they should assist in building up a body of reported cases which will guide shareholders and advisers.[96]

In course of time this will undoubtedly become true. However, it may also produce (as did the case law on the old derivative action) over-cautious judicial decisions. This excessive caution may be most in evidence when public listed companies are the subject of derivative proceedings. In such cases, where the new remedy is most needed, great discouragement may be given at an early stage. As contended earlier, institutional investors

[92] Report, para. 6.73.   [93] Consultation Paper, para. 16.43.
[94] Consultation Paper, para. 16.46.   [95] Consultation Paper, para. 16.44.
[96] Ibid. However, the Consultation Paper elsewhere admits that 'it could be argued that because the factors are not weighted the discretion is so open that the case law will provide little guidance because each case will turn on its own facts'.

meeting a percentage test should be given an easier ride. There is all too great a likelihood that all the old *Foss* v. *Harbottle* judicial attitudes may be reintroduced in the exercise of the new judicial discretion. *De facto* wrongdoer control (the great stumbling block in the *Prudential* litigation) may in a new guise raise once more its obstinate head. In the case of private companies and individual shareholder litigants (where the Consultation Paper's criteria are much more justified), the need for a new statutory derivative action is much less apparent.

It will shortly be seen that the Report is in some ways more restrictive in setting forth the specific matters which 'the court must take . . . into account'.[97] There is also a new specific guideline: 'whether the company in general meeting has resolved not to pursue the cause of action.' This may prove to have a deadly effect in 'choking off' derivative actions.

Threshold test rejected The Report[98] follows the Consultation Paper[99] in recommending that there should be no threshold test on the merits of a case for which leave is sought. The main reason for this is that the inclusion of such an express test would increase the risk of detailed investigation taking place at the leave stage, and that such a 'mini-trial' would be time-consuming and expensive. The Consultation Paper observed that in the Canadian legislation there was no express threshold test,[100] whereas in New Zealand[101] the court must have regard to the likelihood of the proceedings succeeding and the Australian draft legislation[102] provides that there should be a serious question to be tried.

The Report concludes that including a specific threshold test would lead to fine distinctions being drawn as to whether the facts of an individual case fall on the one or on the other side of a particular line drawn. The Report considers this undesirable and that it is better for the courts to develop a principled approach which is not tied to the rigid language of a particular rule or statutory provision.

The 'specific matters' to be considered by the court

Applicants' good faith The Report[103] observes that in any event it is unlikely that a court would grant leave to an applicant whom it considered was acting in bad faith so that it might not be necessary to state

---

[97] See Draft Rule 50.7(2) in Appendix B.   [98] Report, para. 6.71.
[99] Consultation Paper, para. 16.22.
[100] See Appendix G, Canadian Business Corporations Act 1974–75–76, section 239.
[101] See Appendix G, New Zealand Companies Act 1993, section 165(2)(a) and (b). See Watson and Morgan, (1998) 19 *Company Lawyer* 236.
[102] Appendix G, Australian Second Corporate Law Simplification Bill, section 243B(2)(d).
[103] Report, para. 6.75.

this factor specifically. However, the Law Commission takes the view that it was sufficiently important to be mentioned expressly. However, following the Consultation Paper[104] and the views of a majority of consultees, good faith (while it may be taken into account) should not be a prerequisite. The Report also takes the view that 'good faith' should not be defined. While 'extremely difficult to define' it was 'generally readily recognisable'.[105] The Report notes that 'an applicant for leave may benefit commercially if he succeeds in a derivative action and thus has an ulterior motive in bringing it. But nonetheless, the court may consider that he is an appropriate person to bring the action and that the action ought to be brought.'[106]

This relaxed approach to good faith should it is hoped cause no obstacle to an institutional investor or corporate holder of a substantial minority holding in a listed plc from succeeding in an application for leave to bring a derivative action. Such litigants should be encouraged in taking an active approach to enforcing the system of corporate governance established by the Cadbury Report. They should be well able to meet the costs of such litigation. Any compromise or abandonment of derivative proceedings (by institutional investors or any other type of litigant) would of course be subject to the control of the court granting leave.[107]

Interests of the company Following the Consultation Paper,[108] the Report[109] considers that the court should take into account the interests of the company. In doing so the court should have regard to the views of directors on commercial matters. As one of the 'guidelines', the interests of the company is a 'relevant criterion', but the court should not be bound to refuse leave of the proceedings were not in the interests of the company.[110] Thus the court is not bound to accept the views of the directors. The existence of a conflict of interest may affect the weight to be given to them, and the court would give no weight to views which no reasonable director in that position would hold.[111] The Report thus holds firmly to the view that it is not appropriate to require an applicant for leave to prove that the action was in the interests of the company. If this approach were taken, 'it would have the effect of laying down a number of hurdles which an applicant would have to overcome to obtain leave to continue the proceedings, and lead to detailed argument on whether

---

[104] Consultation Paper, para. 16.31.   [105] Report, para. 6.76.   [106] *Ibid.*
[107] Report, para. 6.107.   [108] Consultation Paper, paras. 16.32–16.34.
[109] Report, paras. 6.77–6.79. See Draft Rule 50.7(2)(b) in Appendix B.
[110] Report, para. 6.77.   [111] Report, para. 6.79, footnote 110.

the applicant had (or had not) satisfied' the relevant criteria.[112] On the other hand, where the court is satisfied that the proceedings are not in the interests of the company, there is no good reason why the proceedings should continue, and the court should refuse leave.[113]

This flexible approach should assist a substantial minority shareholder (or group of such) in a public listed company. Institutional investors need to be encouraged to litigate in what they deem is an appropriate case to protect their own investors.

Authorisation and ratification As the Report notes,[114] under the present law if a wrong to the company either has been actually ratified or is *capable* of ratification, it cannot form the basis of a derivative action. The Report refers to the Consultation Paper[115] which explores the lack of clarity and the inconsistencies in the existing case law on ratification. As with other aspects of the existing law of directors' duties, the Report remains determined to 'steer clear' of any attempt at reforming an area of company law beyond its remit. 'There is a danger that our desire to simplify the derivative action could be undermined by the complexities which arise where it is claimed that the relevant breach of duty has been (or may be) ratified.' This approach leads the Law Commission to take a sterner approach to ratification than it does with the 'guidelines' of 'good faith' or the 'interests of the company'. The Report notes[116] that in a number of other Commonwealth jurisdictions the issue of ratification is dealt with by providing that ratification should only be treated as an issue which the court takes into account.[117] The Report takes the somewhat conservative approach that there are serious objections to changing the substantive law of ratification, 'not least because of the uncertainty that this would create in certain commercial situations'.[118]

The Report[119] does, however, make one significant change in the existing common law position. What it calls the 'substantive law' of ratification will remain the same where effective ratification has actually occurred, since 'there will be no subsisting cause of action vested in the company which the shareholder can pursue'. For this purpose, of course, attempted ratification of non-ratifiable breaches of duty will not count. The change introduced is that where a wrong is merely ratifiable it will not prevent a shareholder from commencing a derivative action.

---

[112] Report, para. 6.79.   [113] See Draft Rule 50.8(3) in Appendix B.
[114] Report, para. 6.80.   [115] Consultation Paper, paras. 5.6–5.17.
[116] Report, para. 6.82.
[117] See Consultation Paper, para. 16.36, which refers to legislation in Canada, Australia, Ghana and South Africa. See Appendix G.
[118] Report, para. 6.83.   [119] Report, para. 6.84.

It will still, however, be a factor to which the court has regard. 'Thus, to a small extent, our recommendation represents a change from the position under the common law.'[120] The considerable modesty of this change is given added emphasis by the court's power, in respect of a wrong which is ratifiable but not ratified, to adjourn the proceedings to allow a meeting to be called for the purposes of ratification.[121] If this were not enough, the court may take an alternative approach, if it is clear to the court that the wrong will be ratified and that no purpose will be served in holding a meeting. Here the court can use its discretion to refuse leave for the action to proceed.

This somewhat stultifying approach to minority enforcement of ratifiable breaches of directors' duties is justified in the Report[122] on the ground that the issue of ratification must be left to a 'comprehensive review of directors' duties' while admitting that there may be a case for 'modifying and simplifying the law of ratification'.[123]

The Law Commission's 'minimalist' approach to the shareholders' ratification issue may well undermine much of the good work it has done in framing the new derivative action. The old case law on the distinction between ratifiable and non-ratifiable directors' duties will be kept very much alive. Broadly speaking, it will be as critical to the bringing of the new statutory remedy as it is in the case of the common law derivative action. While it may be right that what the Law Commission calls the 'substantive law of ratification' should continue to dominate the new statutory derivative action in the case of private companies, the ill-attended shareholders' meetings of listed plcs are not an appropriate forum in which carefully weighed decisions about corporate litigation should be made (as the *Prudential* case well illustrates). The applications of the 'twin track' approach to ratification (with or without the use of the power to summon a meeting) could add substantially to the delay, costs and adverse publicity of derivative proceedings. In the case of the common situation in public listed companies where the board exercise *de facto* control, many of the old

---

[120] Report, para. 6.84.

[121] The Report refers to the 'court's power to adjourn to enable the company to call a meeting' at paras. 6.100–6.103.

[122] Report, para. 6.85. The Report pleads that 'the project is only concerned with remedies'.

[123] However, the issue of ratification was also avoided in Law Commission, *Company Directors: Regulating Conflicts of Interest and Formulating a Statement of Duties* (Law Commission Consultation Paper No. 153, 1998). The DTI Company Law Review Steering Group, *Modern Company Law for a Competitive Economy: Developing the Framework* (DTI, URN 00/656, March 2000), para. 4.126, qualified the Law Commission's proposals by requiring ratification by a resolution carried by a sufficient majority of disinterested shareholders. See likewise DTI Company Law Review Steering Group, *Modern Company Law for a Competitive Economy: Final Report* (DTI, URN 01/942 and URN 01/943, July 2001), vol. I, para. 7.46.

problems associated with this situation may return in a new guise. Judicial conservatism may well make such an interpretation of the ratification guideline not unlikely. One casualty may well be that the directors' duty of care and skill may be very difficult to litigate successfully. It must be of some significance that the rigid approach taken to actual ratification has not been adopted in most of the Commonwealth legislation.[124] In particular, the tried and tested Canadian legislation has not justified any fears the Law Commission might have in respect of either private or public companies.[125]

It can at least be contended that in the case of breaches of directors' non-ratifiable duties none of this will present a problem. Thus in the case of fraudulent conduct or misappropriation of corporate assets only the more flexible guidelines of 'good faith' and the 'interests of the company' will operate. This alas does not take account of a further hurdle added by the Report[126] to those proposed in the Consultation Paper.[127]

General meeting resolves not to pursue action Without any meaningful discussion, the Report proposes that, on an application for leave, the court should take account of the fact that the company in general meeting has resolved not to pursue the cause of action. Under the existing law, such a resolution, if made in good faith in what the majority considers to be the benefit of the company, will bind the minority. The Law Commission point out that this is not the same as ratification since the latter has the effect of curing the wrong.[128] Seemingly, this may enable the court, on an application for leave, to bar a derivative action for non-ratifiable breaches of directors' duties as well as ratifiable breaches. Granted the reality of *de facto* control in listed companies, the safeguard of a good faith decision by the majority may prove very inadequate. There may be no way of knowing how adequately informed or carefully considered is the decision of those shareholders who choose to vote in person or by proxy. It is hoped that courts hearing applications for leave will regard this 'guideline' with great care in the case of public listed companies or indeed any company with large numbers of widely scattered shareholders. It is certainly an indication of the greater legal conservatism of the Law Commission's Report as compared with its Consultation Paper. For once, no indication is given of how far the views of consultees influenced

---

[124] See note 100 above.
[125] See Brian Cheffins and Janet Dine, 'Shareholder Remedies: Lessons from Canada' (1992) 13 *Company Lawyer* 89.
[126] Report, paras. 6.87–6.88. See Draft Rule 50.7(2)(d).
[127] Consultation Paper, para. 16.34.
[128] Report, para. 6.87. The Report also points out that it is not the same as taking account of the views of an independent organ. That involves considering the views of a particular group within the company. See Report, paras. 6.89–6.90.

the Law Commission's decision. The main gain of the new remedy could well prove to be enabling very occasional actions to redress fraudulent wrongdoing by directors. Here it is important that such applications for leave should succeed.

Views of independent organ Here the Report[129] follows the Consultation Paper[130] by encapsulating the innovation made by Knox J in *Smith* v. *Croft (No. 2)*[131] that the court should consider the opinion (if any) of an independent organ that, for commercial reasons, the derivative claim should or should not be pursued. Once again, this will be one of the factors that the court should take into account in deciding whether to grant leave.

The term 'independent organ' was used by Knox J to describe a group of persons whose views should be taken account of for the purpose of determining whether a common law derivative action should be allowed to proceed. An 'independent organ' may be described as persons whose votes would not be disregarded on the grounds that they had been (or would be) 'cast with a view to supporting the defendants rather than securing benefit to the company, or that the situation of the person whose vote is considered is such that there is a substantial risk of that happening'.[132] Such an independent majority within the minority must reach its conclusions on grounds genuinely thought to advance the company's interests. Its decision is then treated as that of a 'corporate independent organ' which can properly bar the plaintiff minority shareholders from suing. It is for the judge to determine whether the 'majority within the minority' has fairly reached its decision. It is not his function to say whether his decision is right or wrong.

This is an even more debatable criterion to guide the court as to whether to grant or refuse leave. As a concept 'an independent organ' was not clearly defined in the Consultation Paper[133] and is only vaguely delineated in *Smith* v. *Croft*.[134] The Report[135] confines itself to the observation: 'Knox J made clear that the appropriate independent organ will vary according to the constitution of the company and the identity of the defendants. We consider the courts should be allowed to continue to develop this concept of the independent organ in line with the current authorities.' The dearth of such authorities is part of the problem. The reasoning in *Smith* v. *Croft (No. 2)* might allow not only a 'majority within a minority' but also a 'minority of a minority' to bar proceedings in substantial private companies. In listed plcs an auditor's report (commissioned by the board) should not be a substitute for the right to litigate.

---

[129] Report, paras. 6.88–6.90.   [130] Consultation Paper, para. 16.38.
[131] [1988] Ch 144.   [132] [1988] Ch 144.   [133] Consultation Paper, para. 16.38.
[134] [1988] Ch 144.   [135] Report, para. 6.89.

The judicial detachment of even Cadbury-style non-executive directors is open to question.

In over-cautious or timorous judicial hands, the ability to invoke the 'independent organ' power (in addition to majority shareholders' power) may well enable the worst aspects of the Court of Appeal's decision in *Prudential Assurance Co. Ltd* v. *Newman Industries Ltd (No. 2)*[136] to be resurrected in the exercise of the new statutory discretion to grant leave. In the case of listed plcs this might kill off the use of this remedy at an early stage. If it is to survive such an early 'judicial death', it will be important that the court exercises its discretion in an independent manner, free of the old case law on the derivative action. The 'independent organ' need only be 'taken into account'. It is important that allegations of seriously abusive behaviour should not be defeated by assertions of genuine belief by board members or shareholders who think that litigation must always be the worst option; either financially or in terms of corporate reputation.

Availability of alternative remedies The Report[137] here follows the Consultation Paper[138] and the existing case law[139] in proposing that, in an application for leave, the court should be able to take into account the availability of alternative remedies. However, their availability should not necessarily be conclusive on the issue of the grant of leave. One obvious alternative remedy is an unfair prejudice petition under section 459.[140] The Report[141] makes clear that, while section 459 petitions may to some extent overlap the derivative action,[142] freedom to choose the best remedy or to combine them should remain. However, whether the plaintiff has made the appropriate choice can be taken into account by the court in deciding whether or not to grant leave.

Where, for whatever reasons, an application for leave is refused the rule in *Foss* v. *Harbottle* must be allowed to operate. The Report[143] expresses this in the appropriate doctrinal terms. In the absence of circumstances justifying the grant of leave, 'we consider that the proper plaintiff principle should apply since, in the words of the Court of Appeal in *Prudential*,[144] it "is fundamental to any rational system of jurisprudence"'. While this is obvious, the tone of this observation expresses a desire to

---

[136] [1982] Ch 204.   [137] Report, para. 6.91.
[138] Consultation Paper, paras. 16.39–16.40.
[139] See *Barrett* v. *Duckett* [1995] 1 BCLC 243.   [140] See Chapters 4 and 5 below.
[141] Report, para. 6.11. See Consultation Paper, paras. 16.5–16.6.
[142] Thus section 461(2)(c) provides a means of bringing a derivative action but this has not worked out satisfactorily because the court cannot make an order under section 461(2)(c) unless satisfied that unfair prejudice has occurred.
[143] Report, para. 6.93; Consultation Paper, para. 16.41.   [144] [1982] Ch 204 at 210.

alter substantive company law as little as possible. Many other aspects of the Report's treatment of the new derivative action are plainly influenced by this stance.

The Report rightly follows the common law derivative action in providing that a member cannot bring a derivative action if the company is in liquidation.[145]

The court's ancillary powers in a derivative action

The court's power to adjourn so that the company may call a meeting

The Report[146] retreats from the Consultation Paper's[147] proposal that the court should have power to convene a meeting of the shareholders in order to consider a resolution as to whether the proceedings should be continued. The Consultation Paper also raised for consideration the question of whether the court should have additional powers to determine whether any shareholder should or should not be permitted to vote at the meeting (e.g. a wrongdoing director or shareholder). The Report[148] rejects this latter power as representing a very radical step to 'disenfranchise' a shareholder. It would also involve pre-judging issues before evidence was properly heard. Furthermore, the Report, instead of giving the court power to summon a meeting, confers simply a power to adjourn the hearing of a leave application to enable a meeting of shareholders to be convened for the purpose of considering a resolution affecting a claim.[149] The consequent resolution, in a meeting very likely to be summoned by the board of directors, may 'ratify or release' the relevant cause of action. It is then up to the court to decide on normal principles whether the ratification or release is effective. 'Where the resolution seeks in more general terms to elicit the views of members on whether legal proceedings should be pursued or continued, then the result of the vote will also provide the court with the information it requires (in particular on the views of any "independent organ") without the need for additional powers to alter voting rights.'[150]

Once again, the Report's observation may make good sense in the case of a medium-sized private company. In the case of a large listed plc, especially where the alleged wrongdoers are in *de facto* control or where they have duped a majority of the board of directors, these proposals may

[145] Report, para. 132. See *Gore-Browne on Companies*, para. 28.8.3.
[146] Report, paras. 6.100–6.103.   [147] Consultation Paper, para. 16.49.
[148] The Report rejects the views of a majority of consultees and follows the views of a 'significant number' who expressed reservations.
[149] See Report, para. 6.103; and Draft Rule 50.8(1)(d).   [150] Report, para. 6.102.

produce more fog than light. Many shareholders may fail to attend or to vote by proxy. Those that do so may well have no real knowledge of the substance of the allegations being made or only have a confused grasp. Institutional shareholders and others may respond by 'selling out' if they have not done so already. It may be very difficult for the court to 'read the omens' from a resolution passed by thousands of shareholders with many more simply abstaining. Nevertheless, the court, in hearing the resumed application for leave, may feel obliged to refuse leave since it is required to 'take account' of a resolution not to pursue the cause of action or to take account of the views of an 'independent organ'. If the resolution takes the form of ratifying or releasing the cause of action, the court will have no choice so long as the resolution has been validly passed and the breaches of duty are ratifiable.[151] Once again, the bringing of derivative actions in the case of listed plcs may prove particularly hazardous. It is in such cases, however, that the new statutory derivative action may be most needed, since the existing statutory minority remedies are least appropriate. The vast costs of summoning and holding meetings in the case of public companies is nowhere discussed.

The court's power to substitute claimants or permit discontinuance or compromise of proceedings

The Report[152] makes reasonable provision for the court to allow the substitution of an existing plaintiff in a derivative action by a new plaintiff where this is appropriate. One example given is where the existing plaintiff has some conflict of interest which makes him unsuitable to be a representative plaintiff. The Report proposes that this question could be dealt with under the court's existing powers to add substitute parties.[153]

In most jurisdictions with much experience of derivative action, there are provisions to prevent the plaintiff compromising or abandoning what is after all the company's claim without the leave of the court. The possibilities of collusion with the directors 'buying off' claims is obvious. The Report therefore proposes that the court's leave must be obtained before a derivative action is discontinued or compromised.

Costs indemnity orders

On this topic, the Report[154] has nothing to add. It simply proposes that the courts' powers to make costs indemnity orders in derivative actions

---

[151] See Draft Rule 50.8(4).   [152] Report, para. 6.105.
[153] Reference is made to the Draft Civil Procedure Rules contained in Part 18.
[154] Report, para. 6.104.

should remain unchanged.[155] The assumption that the system of costs indemnity orders strikes the right balance in enabling minority shareholders to bring derivative actions without enormous expense is open to question. In the case of listed public companies, the financial and information barriers still remain formidable. Yet it is in the case of such companies that the need to remove barriers to derivative litigation is most apparent. A recent development across the whole area of civil litigation seems to come too late for the Report.

The powers conferred by section 58 of the Courts and Legal Services Act 1990 enable the Lord Chancellor to provide by statutory instrument that a 'conditional fee agreement shall not be unenforceable by reason only of its being a conditional fee agreement'.[156] As first implemented by the Conditional Fee Agreements Order 1995,[157] enforceable conditional fee agreements were confined to certain specified civil proceedings the object of which was the recovery of a money judgment. This order has been revoked and replaced by the Conditional Fee Agreements Order 1998[158] which applies to *all* civil proceedings (within the scope of section 58) seeking monetary recovery without any exceptions.[159]

This will clearly allow minority shareholders' petitions under section 459 to be financed in this way (assuming appropriate insurance 'cover' can be obtained in the event that the petition is dismissed). A successful section 459 petition will normally produce financial proceeds to meet the terms of the agreement. This may also apply to those 'direct' actions at common law where damages or monetary compensation is or is at least part of the remedy sought. In the case of derivative actions, whether at common law or under the proposed new statutory procedure, this is less clear. Since the proceeds of a derivative action must accrue to the company as nominal defendant, it will inevitably be argued, should the point arise, that it is not open to the plaintiff shareholder in a derivative action to bargain away any part of the proceeds of a successful judgment.

Thus, unless the courts can be persuaded of the need to encourage the bringing of properly funded derivative actions by modifying the normal conceptual analysis of the derivative action, it remains highly likely that

---

[155] As to the existing law, see *Gore-Browne on Companies*, para. 28.9.
[156] Section 58(1) excludes criminal proceedings and specified family proceedings. See sections 58, 58A and 58B of the Courts and Legal Services Act 1990 as amended by the Access to Justice Act 1999.
[157] SI 1995 No. 1674.   [158] SI 1998 No. 1860.
[159] The maximum permitted percentage by which fees may be increased in respect of any proceedings is now 100 per cent. See Conditional Fee Agreements Order 1998 (SI 1998 No. 1860), Article 4. See further *The Ethics of Conditional Fee Agreements* (Society for Advanced Legal Studies, January 2001), paras. 2.29–2.31 as to the effect of the Access to Justice Act 1999.

the only resource open to the prospective plaintiff in a derivative action will be the existing system of costs indemnity orders. These are likely to prove less of an incentive to minority shareholders and their legal advisers.

Remedial procedures rejected by the Report

Several remedial procedures were considered by the Consultation Paper to assist the court hearing a derivative action, which the Report later rejected.

The court's power to appoint an independent expert

Both the Report[160] and the Consultation Paper[161] rejected the idea that the court should have a special power to appoint an expert to investigate and advise on the action along the lines of proposals in the Australian legislation.[162] Such an expert would investigate and report to the court on the financial affairs of the company, the facts or circumstances which gave rise to the cause of action, the subject of the derivative proceedings, and the costs incurred in the proceedings by the parties to the proceedings and the persons granted leave.

No particular reason is given either by the Report or the Consultation Paper for rejecting this idea, except to imply that it is not the 'usual way' in English derivative proceedings. This Australian provision might give the court better and more neutral information than either a resolution in a shareholders' meeting or the views of an allegedly 'independent organ'. In the case of a listed plc it might also prove less expensive than holding a shareholders' meeting.

Pro rata recovery in a derivative action

Both the Report[163] and the Consultation Paper[164] reject the idea of giving so-called *pro rata* relief to individual shareholders in particular cases rather than making the usual order that any damages or other compensation be paid to the company. It is contended that confining any remedy to one in favour of the company fits in with the 'very nature' of a derivative action. It might also encourage 'strike suits', i.e. derivative suits aimed primarily at personal benefit for the plaintiff shareholders. It is difficult to see why there should be objection to relief of this kind in appropriate cases

---

[160] Report, para. 6.99.   [161] Consultation Paper, para. 16.49.
[162] See Consultation Paper, Appendix G, Australian Second Corporate Law Simplification Bill, section 245F(1)(d).
[163] Report, para. 6.108.   [164] Consultation Paper, para. 16.48.

(i.e. where American courts[165] have departed from the general principle of giving relief only to the corporation whose cause of action it is). It is clearly out of the question in most cases (especially *vis-à-vis* listed plcs). There are, however, situations where justice would seem to require judgment in this form. Take as an example the situation where the successful conclusion to a statutory derivative action would hand back the proceeds of judgment to a private company wholly controlled by shareholders actively involved in the wrongdoing to their company (and who are all too likely to repeat the performance). There seems no reason why a plaintiff shareholder should be driven to an unfair prejudice petition if he or she has already chosen to bring a derivative suit.

The Consultation Paper notes that this is often available in the Commonwealth legislation.[166] Thus, despite the reference to the interests of shareholders not party to the proceedings and to the interests of creditors, the court, which has the power to control the abandonment or settlement of derivative suits as well as deciding upon leave to proceed in the first place, should have been given the power to grant *pro rata* recovery in appropriate circumstances in small private companies. Section 459 unfair prejudice petition may not always be appropriate.

Multiple derivative actions

The Consultation Paper[167] examines the need for multiple derivative actions. It notes that businesses are commonly organised in groups of companies consisting, typically of subsidiaries, sub-subsidiaries and associated companies. This gives rise to the issue whether a shareholder in a parent company may bring a derivative action on behalf of a subsidiary or an associated company within the group. Such an action may be appropriate where a shareholder in one company (A) can show that the directors of company A and of a subsidiary (B) or a related company (C) have wrongly prevented the enforcement of a cause of action vested in B or C.

The idea of the 'multiple'[168] derivative suit was first developed in the United States.[169] The Consultation Paper notes that double derivative

---

[165] See *May v. Midwest Refining Co.*, 121 F 2d 431 CCA 1st (1941); *De Tomasso v. Loverro*, 250 App Div 206, 293 NYS 912 (1937).

[166] See Consultation Paper, para. 16.49 which refers to the legislation in New Zealand, Canada and Ghana.

[167] Consultation Paper, para. 16.51.

[168] In America, it is called a 'double derivative suit' if brought by a shareholder of the parent on behalf of a subsidiary and a 'triple derivative suit' if brought on behalf of sub-subsidiary etc. The Consultation Paper prefers the collective term 'multiple' derivative suit.

[169] See, for example, *Kaufman v. Wolfson*, 151 NYS 2d 530 (1950).

suits are available in Canada[170] and multiple derivative actions are available in New Zealand.[171] On the issue of multiple derivative actions, the Consultation Paper left the issue open to the views of consultees and made no provisional recommendation. The Report,[172] even though a small majority of respondents who addressed this issue did consider that provision should be made for multiple derivative actions, rejects the idea. It observes flatly that 'we are not persuaded that it would be helpful or practical to include such a provision'. It is indicated that situations calling for its use are likely to be extremely rare.[173]

The issue is 'left for the courts to resolve, if necessary using the power under section 461(2)(c) of the Companies Act 1985 to bring a derivative action'. This suggestion seems very inappropriate in the case of groups of companies where the ultimate holding company is a listed plc. Once again, the particular needs of such companies are simply not considered or catered for. Provision for multiple derivative actions would be justified in the case of corporate group where a blind eye has been shown by the board, including the chairman and chief executive, towards abuse by directors and managers at a lower level in the group hierarchy. It has been seen that the Report elsewhere excludes any remedy against officers and managers within any company. The negative response of the Law Commission will severely limit the use of the new remedy in the case of groups of companies even where serious fraud and abuse have occurred. In many cases this will not involve the board of the parent company. Breach of the duty of care and skill may be very difficult to establish as against members of the parent company's board who fail to detect more serious breaches of duty at lower levels of this group hierarchy.

Company failing to pursue proceedings

Here the Report[174] for once improves upon the Consultation Paper with a new remedy. The Report is seeking to deal with the situation where the company has commenced an action,[175] but fails to pursue it diligently. It provides that it should be open to shareholders to apply to the court for leave to take over the action and that the court should have to consider the same criteria for leave as those proposed for derivative actions

---

[170] See Appendix A at para. 2.6.
[171] See New Zealand Companies Act 1993, section 165(1) and (2).
[172] Report, para. 6.110.
[173] The DTI Company Law Review Steering Group, *Modern Company Law for a Competitive Economy: Developing the Framework* (DTI, URN 00/656, March 2000) took a different view of multiple derivative actions. See *ibid.*, para. 4.133.
[174] Report, paras. 6.60–6.69.
[175] This must of course be an action for breach of duty by the director.

generally.[176] This right of intervention would not be limited to situations where a minority shareholder had already given notice to bring a derivative action and the company counters this move by commencing its own action – which it subsequently fails to pursue. It would apply to company actions commenced before any procedural step taken by a minority shareholder.[177] The Report proposes that a shareholder should be able to continue, as a derivative action, proceedings commenced by the company which meet the following conditions: (a) the claim is capable of being pursued as a derivative action; (b) the company has failed to prosecute the claim diligently; and (c) the manner in which the company has commenced and continued action amounts to an abuse of the process of the court.[178] On this last point, the Law Commission observes that they consider that an action commenced by a company for the purpose of preventing a shareholder bringing a derivative action, and which it has no real intention of bringing to a conclusion, would amount to abuse of the process of the court.[179]

The Scottish derivative action

As with other chapters in this monograph, the main concern is English law,[180] especially as regards purely procedural matters. In the body of the Report,[181] an explanation is given as to why the almost identical remedy devised by the Scottish Law Commission requires separate treatment. The Scottish Law Commission 'informed' its English equivalent that under Scots law there is no recognised representative or derivative action. A shareholders' right to seek a remedy for the company is conferred by substantive law and not by procedural rules. Amendment of Scots law to introduce a Scottish version of the statutory derivative action requires separate legislative provision.[182] The Scottish Law Commission's consideration of the relevant matters and their proposals (which are very largely the same as those of the English Law Commission) are set out in Appendix D of the Report.[183] Under the Scottish Law Commission's proposals, the new statutory derivative actions will be enacted in full in the form of a new section 458B inserted in the Companies Act 1985.[184]

---

[176] Report, para. 6.60.   [177] Report, para. 6.61.   [178] Report, para. 6.62.
[179] Report, para. 6.63.
[180] Scottish case law of significance is, however, cited where appropriate.
[181] Report, para. 6.22.   [182] Report, para. 6.29.
[183] However, note that the shareholder's individual right of action under Scots law is preserved (para. 73) and a statutory right to seek indemnity out of the company's assets is introduced (para. 71).
[184] See Report, Appendix A; certain procedural rules might, under enabling powers, be altered by the Secretary of State in consultation with the Lord President of the Council.

Conclusions

The Law Commission's recommendations for the new derivative action have obvious advantages over the common law derivative action. In purely procedural terms they are clearly set out in an orderly and logical way in the Draft Rule 50 in Appendix B to the Report. The boundaries with other shareholder remedies are clearly marked out and precise answers are given (in the body of the Report) to most questions that could be raised.

In substantive terms it will enable a minority shareholders' legal advisers contemplating litigation to make a better judgment of the chances of obtaining leave to proceed. Where a non-ratifiable breach of duty is the cause of action, the prospects of success ought to be greater than they are at common law. The ratification bar will not apply, and it is on the whole unlikely that the court will regard a resolution in general meeting that the action should not be pursued as binding upon it. Such a resolution is unlikely to meet the test of good faith. The workings of the 'view of an independent organ' criterion, while remaining obscure, should it is hoped not lead to a refusal of a grant of leave where the director's 'fraud' or misappropriation of assets is alleged.

When it comes to 'ratifiable' breaches of duty, much greater difficulty may be experienced. Where actual ratification has occurred, the court will be bound to refuse leave. Where ratification has not occurred at the time of the application for leave, the other guidelines are bound to present problems. In comparison with the Canadian and most other Commonwealth legislation, the Law Commission's lengthy list of 'relevant matters' seems cautious and conservative. In the Law Commission's view the most important advantage of its list of proposed guidelines is that they should assist in building up a body of reported cases which will guide shareholders and their legal advisers.

In course of time this will undoubtedly become true. However, *de facto* control (the great stumbling block in the *Prudential* litigation) may once more raise its obstinate head, this time in a new guise. One of the great weaknesses of the Law Commission's work on shareholder remedies is its failure even to discuss the problems posed by public listed companies, especially where the board of directors exercise *de facto* control. The various 'guidelines' to be considered by the court granting leave seem most awkward and unsatisfactory in such cases. If the new remedy proves a 'failure' in such cases and succeeds only in the case of private limited

See further the DTI Consultation Paper on Shareholder Remedies (DTI, URN 98/994, November 1998), paras. 3.14–3.16. This Consultation Paper also considers the appropriate court in Scotland to have jurisdiction with regard to the new shareholders' action.

companies, this failure may be linked to the Report's neglect of the need to consider the special problems of listed plcs. It may also produce (as did the case law on the old derivative action) over-cautious judicial decisions. Excessive caution may be most in evidence when public listed companies are the subject of derivative proceedings. In such cases, where the new remedy (at least occasionally) is most needed, great discouragement may be given at an early stage.[185] There is all too great a likelihood that all the *Foss* v. *Harbottle* judicial attitudes may be reintroduced in the exercise of the new judicial discretion.

The Law Commission has very naturally been influenced in many critical areas by the views of its long list of consultees[186] who responded to the Consultation Paper. A glance at this list shows heavy representation of professional advisers and representative bodies whose sympathies are more likely to lie with the directors of companies and listed public companies in particular. Whether the balance is interpreted too far against the minority shareholder with a genuine and serious grievance remains to be seen. The best hope is a judiciary that grasps the need for an effective procedure to give civil remedies their proper place in policing corporate abuse in larger companies. The judiciary's collective power to influence later revisions of 'Draft Part 50: Derivative Claims', if it proves unsatisfactory in practice, also gives some reassurance. A pro-active and vigorous exercise of their discretion to grant leave may make such revision unnecessary.[187]

---

[185] The history of the interpretation by the court of section 210 of the Companies Act 1948 may be repeated.

[186] See Appendix K.

[187] The Company Law Review Steering Group somewhat uncritically endorsed the Law Commission's Report on shareholder remedies in rather general terms. See DTI Company Law Review Steering Group, *Modern Company Law for a Competitive Economy: Developing the Framework* (DTI, URN 00/656, March 2000), paras. 4.65–4.71. This approach is further confirmed in DTI Company Law Review Steering Group, *Modern Company Law for a Competitive Economy: Completing the Structure* (DTI, URN 00/1335, November 2000), para. 5.59. See further DTI Company Law Review Steering Group, *Modern Company Law for a Competitive Economy: Final Report* (DTI, URN 01/942 and URN 01/943, July 2001), vol. I, para. 7.46, which confirms this approach.

4   The statutory minority remedies

Introduction

The Cohen Committee,[1] as long ago as 1945, designed what was to become a statutory remedy against the oppression of minority shareholders
in the form of section 210 of the Companies Act 1948. The Cohen Committee took the view that just and equitable winding up,[2] though it might
be kept in reserve, was usually inappropriate and the derivative action
was frequently unavailable owing to the restrictive nature of the *Foss* v.
Harbottle rule. Even in the current law these observations remain essentially true. It has been seen that the Law Commission has undertaken a
major reform of the derivative action by creating a new statutory derivative remedy. In the case of the minority shareholders' petition for a just
and equitable winding up, it was recast by the House of Lords[3] in 1971,
and has since remained an alternative remedy with some attractive possibilities. In general, however, the courts in recent years have tended to
adapt the unfair prejudice remedy to make it a more suitable remedy for
aggrieved minority shareholders. It will be seen that this does not exclude
resort to petitions seeking a final and equitable winding up, or indeed a
petition which seeks at the outset to combine both remedies.

The Jenkins Committee,[4] when it came to review the oppression remedy created by its predecessor, found its provisions restrictive in various
respects. The Jenkins Committee's proposals for a new 'unfair prejudice'
remedy were, after a long delay, implemented by section 75 of the Companies Act 1980. The most important reform proposed was that the
key concept on which relief should be founded should become 'unfair
prejudice' to shareholders rather than 'oppression'. The significance of
this development will be explored below.[5] The unfair prejudice remedy

---

[1] *Report of the Committee on Company Law Amendment* (Cmd 6659, HMSO, London,
 1945), para. 60.
[2] Under what is now section 122(1)(g) of the Insolvency Act 1986.
[3] See *Ebrahimi* v. *Westbourne Galleries* [1973] AC 360.
[4] *Report of the Company Law Committee* (Cmnd 1749, HMSO, London, 1962).
[5] See p. 94 below.

is now contained in Part XVII of the Companies Act 1985 as amended by the Companies Act 1989.[6]

Because of the intimate link in the development of the two statutory remedies, they are treated together in this chapter. In the chapter that follows,[7] the Law Commission's proposals for reform of the unfair prejudice remedy are explored.[8]

Just and equitable winding up

Ebrahimi v. *Westbourne Galleries*[9] reviewed the nature and scope of the just and equitable ground. This statutory power had existed since the beginning of the registered company (with an even older equitable background). The original wide discretionary power had become much circumscribed with judicial decisions often involving undue technicality. The House of Lords sought to go back to 'first principles' by putting this shareholder remedy on a basis consistent with general equitable principles. At the time of the House of Lords decision in *Westbourne*, its immediate effect was to produce a more amenable and flexible remedy than the existing section 210 of the Companies Act 1948 as it applied to small 'quasi-partnership' type companies. In the course of the intervening thirty years since *Westbourne* was decided, the unfair prejudice remedy provided by sections 459–461 of the Companies Act 1985 has produced an even more attractive remedy for aggrieved minority shareholders. Furthermore, the basic principles set forth in *Westbourne* have been employed to illuminate the meaning of the concept of 'unfair prejudice', as it applies to small private companies.[10]

Lord Wilberforce's exegesis of the meaning of 'just and equitable' in what is now section 122(1)(g) of the Insolvency Act 1986 is of sufficient

---

[6] See sections 459–461 of the Companies Act 1985, as amended by the Companies Act 1989, Schedule 19, para. 11.

[7] See Chapter 5 below, which also considers the self-help remedy proposed for inclusion in Table A.

[8] For a summary of the Commonwealth legislation on 'oppression/unfair prejudice' remedies, see Law Commission, *Shareholder Remedies: A Consultation Paper* (Law Commission Consultation Paper No. 142, Stationery Office, 1996), Appendix 7 at para. 1.9 (Australia), para. 2.7 (Canada), para. 4.9 (New Zealand) and para. 5.9 (South Africa). The terminology usually employed in this legislation combines two alternative concepts, i.e. oppression or unfair prejudice. In the case of South Africa, this becomes 'unfairly prejudicial, unjust or inequitable'. Professor Len Sealy, the Commonwealth editor of *Gore-Browne on Companies* (Jordans, looseleaf), has extensively cited relevant Commonwealth authorities in footnotes 28.12–28.17 (unfair prejudice) and 32.5.7 (just and equitable winding up). See further Chesterman, (1973) 36 *Modern Law Review* 12; and Prentice, (1973) 84 *Law Quarterly Review* 107.

[9] [1973] AC 360.

[10] This development is most evident in the speech of Lord Hoffmann in *O'Neill* v. *Phillips* [1999] 2 BCLC 1 (HL) See p. 96 below.

importance, and has been given such subsequent judicial attention to merit citation at some length.[11]

The words are recognition of the fact that a limited company is a mere legal entity, with a personality in law of its own: that there is room in company law for recognition of the fact that behind it, or among it, there are individuals, with rights, expectations and obligations *inter se* which are not necessarily submerged in the company structure. That structure is defined by the Companies Act 1948 and by the articles of association by which the shareholders agree to be bound. In most companies and in most contexts, this definition is sufficient and exhaustive, equally so whether the company is large or small. The 'just and equitable' provision does not, as the respondents suggest, entitle one party to disregard the obligation he assumes by entering a company, nor the court to dispense him from it. It does, as equity always does, enable the court to subject the exercise of legal rights to equitable considerations; considerations, that is, of a personal character arising between one individual and another, which may make it unjust, or inequitable, to insist on legal rights, or to exercise them in a particular way. It would be impossible, and wholly undesirable, to define the circumstances in which these considerations may arise. Certainly, the fact that a company is a small one, or a private company, is not enough. There are very many of these where the association is a purely commercial one, of which it can safely be said that the basis of association is adequately and exhaustively laid down in the articles. The superimposition of equitable considerations requires something more, which typically may include one, or probably more, of the following elements: (i) an association formed or continued on the basis of a personal relationship, involving mutual confidence – this element will often be found where a pre-existing partnership has been converted into a limited company; (ii) an agreement, or understanding, that all, or some (for there may be 'sleeping' members), of the shareholders shall participate in the conduct of the business; (iii) restriction upon the transfer of the members' interest in the company – so that if confidence is lost, or one member is removed from management, he cannot take out his stake and go elsewhere.

Lord Wilberforce emphasised that the mere fact that the exclusion of a director from participation in a company accords with the powers conferred on a majority in general meeting by section 303 of the Companies Act 1985 to remove directors from the board, or that what has happened is consistent with the articles, does not prevent the court's intervention on the just and equitable ground. The effect of section 122(1)(g) of the Insolvency Act 1986 is to enable the court 'to subject the exercise of legal rights to equitable considerations' etc. The passage cited above indicates that Lord Wilberforce declined to define in an exhaustive manner the circumstances in which the court might invoke this principle of subjecting legal rights to 'equitable considerations'.

The expulsion from participation in management indicated by criteria (i) to (iii) in the passage quoted (on which the appeal in *Westbourne* was

[11] See [1973] AC 360 at 379–80.

decided) is a description of the type of situation which would typically give rise to the subjection of legal rights or powers to equitable considerations.

The primary importance of the decision of the House of Lords in *Westbourne* is to reject the view of the Court of Appeal in that case that the petitioner must prove that the exclusion was not *bona fide* in the interests of the company or such that no reasonable man could consider it to be in the interests of the company. Clearly, the 'underlying obligation in good faith and confidence' which justifies intervention does not require proof of bad faith. As earlier case law already indicated, expulsion from participation in management justified the application of the 'just and equitable' provision where the expulsion resulted in the loss of participation in profits and left the expelled petitioner as a locked-in shareholder.[12]

The application of the above principles to situations *not* involving expulsion remains to some degree uncertain. They have been applied to joint venture companies which did not strictly come within the 'quasi-partnership' criteria.[13] It has also been indicated judicially that the retention of profits which excludes members (not involved in management) from participation by way of dividend will justify a winding up order where this defeats the members' expectations and leaves the petitioner unable to realise the full value of his or her shares.[14] It may be that any course of dealing which produces a breakdown in mutual confidence might suffice to justify the making of a winding up order under section 122(1)(g) unless that breakdown in mutual confidence is referable to the conduct of the complainant shareholders.[15] It would seem that the loss of confidence need not be mutual.[16] The old cases where deadlock in management was held to justify a winding up order must now be brought within this principle even though it cannot be said to be the fault of the respondent rather than the petitioner. There are other situations where the grant of just and equitable winding up was not based on expulsion from management. These cases, though somewhat unlikely to be invoked today, appear not to be overruled by the House of Lords decision in *Westbourne*. The case law on loss of 'substratum' and on 'fraudulent and illegal companies'[17]

---

[12] See *Lewis v. Haas*, 1971 SLT 157 (Court of Session); and *Re Davis & Collett* [1935] Ch 593.

[13] See *Re A&BC Chewing Gum* [1975] 1 WLR 579; and *Re Abbey Leisure Ltd* [1990] BCLC 342 (CA).

[14] *Re A Company (No. 00370 of 1987), ex parte Glossop* [1988] 1 WLR 1068. Lord Cross of Chelsea in *Westbourne* also considered the application of these principles to the refusal by the board of a share transfer.

[15] See *Jesner v. Jarrad Properties Ltd* [1993] BCLC 1032 (Court of Session); *Vujnovich v. Vujnovich* [1990] BCLC 227 (PC).

[16] See *Re Yenidje Tobacco Co.* [1916] 2 Ch 246 (CA); *Re Sailing Ship Kenternere Co.* (1897) WN 58; and *Re American Pioneer Leather Co.* [1918] 1 Ch 556.

[17] See *Gore-Browne on Companies*, para. 32.5.

is indicative that the power to decree a just and equitable winding up has a wider ambit than the unfair prejudice remedy under section 459. The relationship between these two statutory remedies is further explored below.[18]

The concept of unfair prejudice

Section 459(1) of the Companies Act 1985 allows a member to apply to the court by petition for an order under the section. The ground on which he or she may petition (and on which the court must be satisfied that the petition is well founded[19]) is as follows: that the company's affairs are being conducted in a manner which is unfairly prejudicial to the interests of its members generally[20] or of some part of the members (including at least the petitioner) or that any actual or proposed act or omission on its behalf would be so prejudicial.[21]

The concept of unfair prejudice still remains a matter of contention even if its meaning is less elusive than once was the case. It is perhaps better characterised not so much as an analytical concept but rather as a general standard to guide the court as to what kind or degree of misbehaviour or mismanagement should justify the court, on hearing a petition under section 459, in exercising its powers of intervention under section 461. Before Lord Hoffmann's speech in the House of Lords decision in *O'Neill* v. *Phillips*,[22] which will be further considered below, a flexible and somewhat open-ended concept of unfair prejudice had been developed by the courts. This deserves separate examination before turning to Lord Hoffmann's attempted 'restatement' of the earlier law. This case law still provides a sound basis for the many and varied applications of the jurisdiction conferred by section 459.

The following passage from the judgment of Slade J,[23] later cited with approval by Nourse J in *Re RA Noble (Clothing) Ltd*,[24] gave this explanation of the term 'unfair prejudice':

I do not think it necessary or appropriate in this judgment to attempt any comprehensive exposition of the situations that may give rise to the court's jurisdiction under section 75. Broadly, however, I would say this. Without prejudice to the generality of the wording of the section, which may cover many other situations,

---

[18] See p. 102 below.
[19] See section 461(1). See *Re A Company (No. 004175 of 1986)* [1987] 1 WLR 585.
[20] Section 459(1), as amended by the Companies Act 1989, Schedule 19.
[21] As to the procedural requirements in respect of petitions under section 459, see p. 109 below.
[22] [1999] 2 BCLC 1 (HL).   [23] *Re Bovey Hotels*, unreported, 31 July 1981.
[24] [1983] BCLC 273 at 290–1. The passage quoted in the text was cited with approval by Ralph Gibson LJ in *Re A Company (No. 002470 of 1988), ex parte Nicholas* [1992] BCC 895 at 910. See also *Re Sam Weller & Sons Ltd* [1990] BCLC 80 at 85–90.

a member of a company will be able to bring himself within the section if he can show that the value of his shareholding in the company has been seriously diminished or at least seriously jeopardised by reason of a course of conduct on the part of those persons who have had *de facto* control of the company, which is unfair to the members concerned. The test of fairness must, I think, be an objective, not a subjective one. In other words, it is not necessary for the petitioner to show that persons who have had *de facto* control of the company have acted as they did in the conscious knowledge that this was unfair to the petitioner or that they were acting in bad faith; the test I think is whether a reasonable bystander observing the consequences of their conduct would regard it as having unfairly prejudiced the petitioner's interests.[25]

It is hardly surprising that the replacement of 'oppressive conduct' (in the old section 210) by 'unfair prejudice' was given its intended effect at an early stage by the judiciary. 'Bad faith' and 'lack of probity' (and their associated burden of proof) were now irrelevant. Similarly, the use or threatened use of the majority shareholders' voting power is not a requirement. The term 'unfair prejudice' is a relatively more objective one which is concerned with the running of the company (or particular acts of misbehaviour) that are clearly unfair in their consequences to the complaining shareholder, even if the respondents have acted in the best good faith. It is also clear that the judge retains considerable discretion as to how this concept is applied to the widely varying sets of circumstances that arise in corporate disputes that lead to section 459 petitions.

The test of the 'reasonable bystander' (obviously a metaphor for the function of the judge) may well no longer be acceptable, but the other elements in the passage cited above seem to remain a sound description of the modern case law on unfair prejudice. In particular, the rejection of 'bad faith' can hardly be questioned.[26] It will be seen that Lord Hoffmann's emphasis on the idea of 'good faith' in carrying out the corporate contract as the essence of unfair prejudice appears to raise a difficult problem of analysis.

At an early stage the courts made clear that the petitioner does not have to establish the infringement of a shareholder's right under company law. The concept of unfairness cuts across the distinction between acts which do or do not infringe rights attaching to shares.[27] Nothing in Lord Hoffmann's speech in *O'Neill* v. *Phillips*,[28] with its emphasis on 'contractualism', contradicts this principle. It will be seen that Lord Hoffmann's references to wider equitable principles applicable to the expectation of members in 'quasi-partnership' companies makes this clear.

---

[25] [1983] BCLC 273 at 290–1.   [26] See p. 98 below.
[27] See *Re A Company (No. 008695 of 1985)* (1986) 2 BCC 99, 024; *McGuinness* v. *Bremner plc* [1988] BCLC 673 (Court of Session).
[28] [1999] 2 BCLC 1. See p. 96 below.

On the other hand, the plain infringement of a shareholder's right (e.g. to be given accurate accounting information as prescribed by the Companies Act 1985) can be the ground of an allegation of unfair prejudice.[29]

This is well founded in the wording in section 459(1) which refers not only to conduct but also to where 'any actual or proposed act or omission on its behalf would be so prejudicial'. As far as prejudicial conduct is concerned, it is clear that the conduct complained of must relate to the manner in which the company's affairs are conducted. Thus the non-payment of debts owed by a holding company to its subsidiary (where this was an attempt to keep the group afloat in financial difficulties) has been held not to constitute unfair prejudice in the conduct of the subsidiary's affairs.[30] Such 'conduct' does not include acts of a shareholder carried out in a personal capacity outside the course of the company's business.[31] Similarly, where the respondent refused to sell his shares, this is a private matter and is no part of the conduct of the company's affairs.[32]

'Unfair prejudice' in the House of Lords

In *O'Neill* v. *Phillips*,[33] the House of Lords has for the first time had an opportunity to consider the scope of the 'unfair prejudice' remedy. Lord Hoffmann gave the only reasoned judgment. The case concerned a building construction company whose original 'proprietors' first allowed the petitioner, an employee, a minority holding and a directorship. Later he was left alone on the board as *de facto* managing director. Subsequent changes included a profit-sharing agreement. Some of these profits were later capitalised by the issue of non-voting shares. Discussions took place with a view to the petitioner obtaining a 50 per cent shareholding but no agreement was, in the event, concluded. In a later building recession, the company's position worsened. The petitioner was excluded from managing the company. The profit-sharing arrangement was later terminated and the petitioner left the company and brought a section 459 petition. The trial judge dismissed his petition but it succeeded in the Court of Appeal.[34] The respondent appealed to the House of Lords.

[29] See e.g. *Re A Company (No. 000789 of 1987), ex parte Shooter* [1990] BCLC 384; and *Re A Company (No. 005134 of 1986), ex parte Harries* [1989] BCLC 383 (breach of statutory pre-emptive rights). Cf. *Re A Company (No. 005685 of 1988) (No. 2), ex parte Schwartze* [1989] BCLC 427.

[30] *Nicholas* v. *Soundcraft Electronics* [1993] BCLC 360.

[31] *Re A Company (No. 001761 of 1986)* [1987] BCLC 141.

[32] *Re Legal Costs Negotiators Ltd* [1999] 2 BCLC 171 (CA).

[33] [1999] 2 BCLC 1.   [34] [1997] 2 BCLC 739.

Lord Hoffmann's exegesis of 'unfair prejudice' in section 459(1), as in his earlier Court of Appeal judgment in *Re Saul D Harrison & Sons plc*,[35] relies on two essential points. These are the fundamentally promissory nature of the basis on which relief may be granted, and, secondly, that the same principles underlie both the just and equitable winding up remedy and the unfair prejudice remedy.

As regards the first point, he observes[36] that a member of a company will not ordinarily be entitled to complain of unfairness unless there has been some breach of the terms on which he agreed that the affairs of the company be conducted. These terms are contained in the articles of association and sometimes in the collateral agreements made between shareholders.

In a quasi-partnership company, there will usually be understandings between the members at the time they entered into the association. But there may be later promises, by words or conduct, which it would be unfair to allow a member to ignore. Nor is it necessary that such promises should be independently enforceable as a matter of contract. A promise may be binding as a matter of justice and equity. Although for one reason or another . . . it would not be enforceable in law.[37]

Lord Hoffmann relies strongly on Lord Wilberforce's *locus classicus* in *Ebrahimi* v. *Westbourne Galleries*[38] to underpin the second point: there will be cases in which equitable considerations make it unfair for those conducting the affairs of the company to rely upon their strict legal powers. 'This unfairness may consist in a breach of the rules or in using rules in a manner which equity would regard as contrary to good faith.'[39] Lord Hoffmann traces the principles upon which the court decides that the alleged conduct is unjust, inequitable or unfair back to nineteenth-century cases such as *Bisset* v. *Daniel*[40] and the distinction between the legal and equitable approach to the use of powers.

Lord Hoffmann is clearly aware of drawing too close an analogy between 'just and equitable' winding up and the notion of unfairness in section 459. He observes that 'the parallel I have drawn . . . does not mean that conduct will not be unfair unless it would have justified an order to wind up the company'. He later adds: 'The parallel is not the conduct which the court will treat as justifying a particular remedy but the principles upon which it decides that the conduct is unjust, inequitable or unfair.'[41] The difficulty with this approach is that it does not make

---

[35] [1995] 1 BCLC 14 at 19–20.   [36] [1999] 2 BCLC 1 at 8.   [37] *Ibid.* at 10–11.
[38] [1973] AC 360 at 379.   [39] [1999] 2 BCLC 1 at 8.
[40] (1853) 10 Hare 493; 68 ER 1022.   [41] [1999] 2 BCLC 1 at 9.

it sufficiently clear that a just and equitable winding up order may be made in circumstances of a breakdown in mutual confidence where it is impossible to hold that the respondent has acted unfairly. The most obvious example (well established before *Westbourne* but not changed by it) is where there is deadlock between corporate partners which they are incapable of resolving.

Lord Hoffmann's use of the term 'good faith' (to cover it seems both 'just and equitable' and 'unfairness') is perhaps unfortunate. In *Westbourne* the House of Lords[42] specifically rejected the test of 'bad faith' as the basis for a just and equitable winding up and overruled the Court of Appeal on the issue. The petitioners need not show bad faith in the sense that the respondents had not acted in good faith in the company's interests. In the case of section 459 petitions, it is well established that a breach of directors' duties[43] may enable the court to find unfair prejudice. It is clear that a breach of fiduciary duties, even if the breach does not involve bad faith, may in appropriate circumstances justify relief under section 459. It is thus difficult to grasp in what more generic sense the term 'good faith' is employed.[44]

Certainly, Lord Hoffmann's judgment elsewhere makes clear that 'exercising rights in breach of some promise or undertaking' is not the only form of conduct which will be regarded as 'unfair for the purposes of section 459. For example, there may be some event which puts an end to the basis upon which the parties entered into association with each other, making it unfair that one shareholder should insist upon the continuance of the association.' Thus Lord Hoffmann's observations on the term 'unfair prejudice' are valuable as a conceptual analysis. It is debatable whether they have the full weight of the *ratio decidendi* of a House of Lords decision. His observations do not amount to a restatement of the pre-existing body of case law. Earlier decisions are not overruled. It neither extends nor restricts the range of circumstances which may amount to unfair prejudice.

In a number of other more specific matters the decision in *O'Neill* v. *Phillips* is, however, both clarificatory and innovative. These will be examined later.

Jonathan Parker J in *Re Guidezone*[45] came to the firm conclusion that the jurisdiction to make a winding up order is no wider than the jurisdiction

---

[42] [1973] AC 360 at 379. It has also been rejected as the test of unfair prejudice. See *Gore-Browne on Companies*, para. 28.13.2.

[43] See *Gore-Browne on Companies*, para. 28.13.7. Lord Hoffmann's earlier judgments have been important on this point. Lord Hoffmann draws an analogy to 'continental systems' which introduce a general requirement of good faith in contractual performance.

[44] [1999] 2 BCLC 1 at 9.   [45] [2000] 2 BCLC 321 at 357.

to grant relief under section 459: 'it would in my judgment be extremely unfortunate, and inconsistent with the approach and the reasoning of Lord Hoffmann in *O'Neill* v. *Phillips* if, given the two parallel jurisdictions, conduct which is not "unfair" for the purposes of section 459 should nevertheless be capable of founding a case for a winding up order on the just and equitable ground.' Though this may make sound policy sense, it ignores a more qualified distinction in Lord Hoffmann's speech noted earlier. 'The parallel is not the conduct which the court will treat as justifying a particular remedy but the principles upon which the court decides that the conduct is unjust, inequitable and unfair.'[46] It has also been observed that the earlier case law on just and equitable winding up (subsumed in *Westbourne*), notably the cases on deadlock, cannot be predicated on an 'objective' notion of 'unfairness'. The petitioner does not have to establish that the respondents' conduct is unjust and inequitable. It has been held, however, that the 'clean hands' defence (as regards the petitioner's misconduct) applies to a just and equitable winding up but not to an unfair prejudice petition.[47] The proposition (in Lord Hoffmann's speech in *O'Neill*) that 'company law has developed seamlessly from the law of partnership which was treated by equity, like the Roman *societas*, as a contract of good faith' is difficult to square with Lord Wilberforce's well-known observations that 'a small company, however small, however domestic, is a company not a partnership not even a quasi-partnership and it is through the just and equitable clause that obligations, common to partnership relations, may come in'.[48]

Jonathan Parker J cites Lord Hoffmann in respect of the need for clear basic principles which still preserve a flexible judicial discretion: 'a balance has to be struck between the breadth of discretion given to the court and the principle of legal certainty.'[49] This does not warrant a total conflation of just and equitable winding up and unfair prejudice petitions (i.e. as to the ground of relief). The statutory concept of unfair prejudice did not exist when the House of Lords decided *Westbourne*. The invocation of generalised notions of 'established equitable principles' or 'acting in a manner which equity would regard as contrary to good faith',[50] fails to resolve the question (still left open in *O'Neill*) as to how far it is proper to distinguish the basis for judicial intervention in the two statutory remedies. It may be true that it is desirable as a matter of policy to prevent 'transferring business from the section 459 jurisdiction to the winding up

---

[46] [1999] 2 BCLC 1 at 9. See further Stephen Acton, 'Just and Equitable Winding Up: The Strange Case of the Disappearing Jurisdiction' (2001) 22 *Company Lawyer* 134.
[47] *Re London School of Electronics* [1986] Ch 211 at 227.
[48] [1973] AC 360 at 380.   [49] [1999] 2 BCLC 1 at 8.
[50] [2000] 2 BCLC 321 at 356.

jurisdiction',[51] but this does not itself deal with the problems raised by the case law. Doubtless this question will be revisited by the courts in the future.[52]

Varied applications of the remedy

One of the most significant areas of application of the unfair prejudice remedy is that of directors' duties. To some extent it can be a substitute for the derivative action even though the two remedies are clearly different in character. In an unfair prejudice petition *de facto* control by the wrongdoer may suffice.[53] The issue of ratification will not necessarily clearly determine the application of the remedy.[54] In three cases decided in 1986,[55] Hoffmann J, in rejecting strike-out applications, clearly established that allegations of breach of fiduciary duty were capable of establishing unfair prejudice to minority shareholders in a private company or a small unlisted public company. These cases make it clear that even if the facts alleged would warrant the bringing of a derivative action this will not bar a petition. This can apply to fiduciary duties not to mislead shareholders when making statements supporting one of two rival takeover bids. It also applies to fraudulently inducing the petitioner to sell the shares in a private company to a public company as part of a manifestly dishonest scheme. It can also apply to misappropriation of corporate assets. It was emphasised that the interests of a member are not limited to his or her strict legal rights since the use of the word 'unfairly' enables the court to have regard to wider equitable considerations.[56]

In the case of directors' negligence the courts have adopted a more cautious approach. Here there is a divergence between the common law duty of care owed by directors to their company[57] and the allegations of

---

[51] [2000] 2 BCLC 321 at 351.

[52] See further, as to reported cases where Lord Hoffmann's speech in *O'Neill* v. *Phillips* has been relied upon, *Arrow Nominees* v. *Blackledge* [2000] 2 BCLC 167 at 177; *Re Benfield Greig Group plc* [2000] 2 BCLC 488 at 507; *Profinance Trust SA* v. *Gladstone* [2000] 2 BCLC 516 at 525; *Brownlow* v. *GH Marshall Ltd* [2000] 2 BCLC 655 at 673–4; *West* v. *Blanchet* [2000] 1 BCLC 795 at 804; and *North Holdings Ltd* v. *Southern Tropics Ltd* [1999] 2 BCLC 625 at 633–4 (CA). These cases, while accepting the authority of Lord Hoffmann's speech, add little to it by way of analysis or exegesis.

[53] *Re RA Noble Clothing* [1983] BCLC 273.

[54] See *Fexuto Pty Ltd* v. *Bosnjak Holdings Pty Ltd* (1998) 28 ACSR 689 (Supreme Court of New South Wales).

[55] *Re A Company (No. 005278 of 1985)* [1986] 1 WLR 281; *Re A Company* [1986] BCLC 382; *Re A Company* [1986] BCLC 376.

[56] *Re A Company* [1986] BCLC 376; *McGuinness* v. *Bremner plc* 1988 SLT 891. See further *Re A Company, ex parte Burr* [1992] BCLC 724; and *Re Ghyll Beck Driving Range Ltd* [1993] BCLC 1126.

[57] See *Gore-Browne on Companies*, para. 27.19. The common law duty has been raised to a more demanding standard.

gross mismanagement required to support a finding of unfair prejudice. In *Re Elgindata*,[58] Warner J was of the view that the court would ordinarily be very reluctant to treat managerial decisions as unfairly prejudicial conduct. Nevertheless, he indicated that it would be open to the court in an appropriate case to find that serious mismanagement of a company's business could constitute unfair prejudice. Disagreement between the parties as to whether a particular management decision is commercially sound is clearly not enough. In effect a distinction has to be made between a breach of duty by a director and serious and persistent mismanagement. An example would be 'where the majority shareholders, for reasons of their own, persisted in retaining in charge of the management of the company's business a member of their family who was demonstrably incompetent.[59] This divergence in enforcing standards of managerial competence makes the significance of the proposed statutory derivative action of great importance.[60]

A similar diversity of approach can be found between derivative proceedings and unfair prejudice petitions in respect of public listed companies. In the case of derivative suits there is in principle no conceptual problem about bringing proceedings against a listed company. It was seen[61] that the 'hurdle' of wrongdoers' control may present practical difficulties, but beyond that the derivative action applies to any type of company. In the case of unfair prejudice petitions the matter is more complex. In its original form (prior to amendment by the Companies Act 1989) in section 459, the words 'the interests of some part of the members (including at least himself)' were held to make relief under section 459 more difficult in the case of public listed companies. Conduct that was unfairly prejudicial to all the members could not be comprehended.[62] This conduct that damaged the interests of all shareholders (including those shares held by wrongdoing directors who still gained advantages by their breach of duty) could not qualify. Later decisions gave a more qualified interpretation in respect of the non-payment of dividends. Even if the rights of all the members were affected equally by the allegedly unfairly prejudicial conduct, the interests of some part of the members may be affected in a way that was unfairly prejudicial to them.[63] This judicial difference of interpretation was resolved by the amended version of section 459: 'unfairly prejudicial to the interests of its members generally

[58] [1991] BCLC 959 at 993.
[59] *Ibid.* at 993, applied in *Re Macro (Ipswich) Ltd* [1994] 2 BCLC 354.
[60] See Chapter 3 above.   [61] See Chapter 2, p. 27 above.
[62] *Re A Company (No. 00370 of 1987), ex parte Glossop* [1988] 1 WLR 1068 at 1074 *per* Harman J.
[63] *Re Sam Weller & Sons Ltd* [1990] Ch 682.

or some part of the members.'[64] Thus as a matter of basic principle misconduct in listed public companies affecting the shareholders may be the
subject of an unfair prejudice petition. The real limitation, as will be indicated below,[65] is that such companies cannot fall within the arena of
'legitimate expectations'. In particular, it will be seen that City regulations
(the Combined Code, etc.) have no bearing on the matter.

Another perhaps more fundamental limitation in the case of public
listed companies is that the overwhelmingly usual remedy sought under
section 461 (a 'buy-out' of the petitioner's shares) makes little practical sense in the case of a public listed company, particularly where all the
shareholders are affected. In such companies the courts' power under
section 461 to allow the petitioner to bring proceedings on behalf of the
company has relevance. This unusual form of statutory derivative action,
it will be seen, is rarely ever invoked. The remedy thus remains largely
stultified in the case of large public companies. Clearly, however, there is
no reason why it should not be invoked where shareholders' rights under
the articles have been infringed, or class rights in the articles have been
improperly altered. As was noted earlier,[66] section 459 may provide a
useful alternative to *Foss* v. *Harbottle* proceedings in such cases. Here the
remedy appropriate under section 461 may be the power to regulate the
conduct of the company's affairs in future,[67] and the power to 'require
the company to refrain from doing or continuing an act complained of
by the petitioner or to do an act which the petitioner has complained it
has omitted to do'.[68]

Choice of remedies

In the case of small private companies it has been seen that there is
considerable overlap (in terms of availability and application) between the
two statutory minority remedies. There is also the question of a provision
in the articles allowing the purchase of the minority's shares, usually
on the basis of the auditor's valuation. The courts have given careful
consideration to the factors involved in this choice. It is not by any means
a free choice open to the minority shareholder or his or her legal advisers.

---

[64] Companies Act 1989, Schedule 19, para. 11.   [65] See p. 111 below.

[66] See Chapter 2 above. For two contrasting views on the likely availability of section
459 petitions where the shareholders generally are affected, see Brian Cheffins and
Janet Dine, (1992) 13 *Company Lawyer* 89; and Stephen Griffiths, (1992) 13 *Company
Lawyer* 83.

[67] Section 461(2)(a). See further below.

[68] Section 461(2)(b). See *Re Whyte (Petitioner)* 1984 SLT 156; *McGuinness* v. *Black* 1990
SLT 156. See also *Re A Company* [1985] BCLC 80, *Re Mountforest* [1993] BCC 509.

The main restriction on choice of remedies is what is known as the 'alternative remedy' provision in section 125(2) of the Insolvency Act 1986 which defines the conditions on which a just and equitable winding up order must be based. Section 125(2) first requires that the petitioner must be entitled to relief either by winding up or by some other means, and that in the absence of some other remedy it would be just and equitable that the company should be wound up. This latter provision is then made subject to this important proviso: the remedy is not to apply 'if the court is also of the opinion both that some other remedy is available to the petitioner and [that] they are acting unreasonably in seeking to have the company wound up instead of pursuing the other remedy'. This 'alternative remedy' provision (as it is usually called) became even more important when section 459 became a more inclusive remedy both substantively and in terms of the remedial orders that might be made. These are obviously more satisfactory than the 'sledgehammer' outcome of a successful petition under section 122(1)(g) of the Insolvency Act 1986.[69]

As the discussion of the concept of unfair prejudice earlier in this chapter shows, there is no complete overlap between the two remedies.[70] Thus there is no requirement that the petitioner come to court with 'clean hands' in the case of an unfair prejudice petition.[71] In general terms this defence does apply to a just and equitable winding up.[72] However, even in respect of unfair prejudice proceedings the petitioner's misconduct may render the conduct complained of, even if prejudicial, not unfair. It may also affect the relief granted by the courts even where unfair prejudice is established.[73]

It is now appropriate to consider to what extent an offer to buy the petitioner's shares may be a bar to either a winding up petition or to an unfair prejudice petition.

The offer to buy as a bar to a winding up

A reasonable offer to buy out the petitioner's shares at a fair price (with appropriate expert valuation) may suffice. In *Re A Company (No. 002567*

---

[69] See *Practice Direction (Company Court: Contributors Petition)* [1990] 1 WLR 490. This draws practitioners' attention to the undesirability of including as a matter of course a petition for winding up as an alternative to an order under section 459. This should only be done if winding up is the relief the petitioners prefer or if it is considered to be the only relief to which they are entitled.

[70] See p. 94 above.   [71] *Re London School of Electronics* [1986] Ch 211.

[72] But see *Vujnovich* v. *Vujnovich* [1990] BCLC 227 (PC).

[73] See *Re London School of Electronics* [1986] Ch 211 at 222.

of 1982),[74] Vinelott J observed that the jurisdiction under what is now section 125(2) is discretionary. The court would be at least entitled to refuse to make a winding up order if satisfied that the petitioner was persisting in asking for such an order, and that it would be unfair to the other shareholders to make that order having regard to any offer they made to the petitioner to meet his grievance in another way. The petitioner was also held to have acted unreasonably in refusing to accept the respondent's offer to purchase his shares at a valuation. The date when the adequacy of the respondent's offer has to be determined is the date of the hearing and not that of the presentation of the petition. It is as much an abuse of the process of the court to persist in a petition which, because of a subsequent offer, is bound to fail as it would be to present a petition which on the facts existing at the time of presentation is bound to fail. This gives the respondents, faced with a petition under section 122(1)(g) every incentive to negotiate an adequate offer to buy out the petitioner by means of a fair and independent valuation, i.e. where no price can be agreed. To make sure the respondent continued to show sincerity until the completion of the 'buy-out', Vinelott J decided not to dismiss the petition outright. It was merely 'stood over' to enable the parties to agree the terms of submission to an arbitration or valuation by an expert. When agreement was reached, 'the matter could be mentioned to the court and the petition stayed'. If there was any disagreement, Vinelott J continued, he would 'then hear further argument'.

Whenever possible it would seem, a winding up order with all its potential for the destruction of an otherwise viable business and with harsh consequences for the innocent employees will be denied whenever a viable alternative remedy is available. In the *Re A Company* case before Vinelott J referred to above, the court rejected the argument that in a small quasi-partnership type company the petitioner is entitled to reject an alternative 'buy-out' remedy on the ground that (as in partnership law) he is entitled to a share of 'partnership' assets on their realisation. The only qualification to this proposition admitted by Vinelott J was that, where the petitioner (excluded from a quasi-partnership despite the underlying assumption of a right to participate) has always insisted on a winding up as the only remedy, then the argument that he was entitled to that remedy might have succeeded. On the facts of this case that was not so. From the time of exclusion from participation, the petitioner had indicated a willingness to sell to his co-shareholders at a fair price to be negotiated.

---

[74] *Re A Company (No. 002567 of 1982)* [1983] 1 WLR 927. See also *Re Copeland & Craddock Ltd* [1997] BCC 294 (CA): a petitioner was allowed to proceed in the hope of bidding for the business when it was sold by the liquidator.

The principle so firmly stated in these first-instance decisions on the alternative remedy was reviewed by the Court of Appeal in *Virdi* v. *Abbey Leisure*.[75] Where a petitioner is entitled in principle to a just and equitable winding up, an offer by the respondent majority shareholders to buy his shares, under a provision in the articles, at a fair value to be agreed by an accountant, could reasonably be refused by the petitioner. The trial judge was held to be wrong in the exercise of his discretion under section 125(2) in deciding to strike out the petition. The Court of Appeal accepted that an accountant acting under the procedure in the articles would value them on a discounted basis as a minority holding. The petitioner was entitled to insist on his normal right to a *pro rata* valuation, which would result from an order for a just and equitable winding up. Balcombe LJ[76] observed that the courts have shown a general inclination, under both sections 459 and 122(1)(g), towards a valuation on a *pro rata* basis. Balcombe LJ also stressed that, in a just and equitable winding up based on the principles laid down by the House of Lords in *Ebrahimi* v. *Westbourne Galleries*,[77] legal rights and obligations conferred or imposed on shareholders by the constitution of the company may be subject to equitable considerations. This freed the petitioner from his obligation under the articles.[78]

The offer to buy as a bar to an unfair prejudice petition

In a number of cases,[79] the courts have stressed that, where there is an irretrievable breakdown which is the fault of neither petitioner nor respondent, pre-emptive rights provisions in the articles should be sought rather than a petition under section 459 on the ground of unfair prejudice. Where the court concludes that unfair prejudice to the petitioner could not be established at a full hearing, this is obviously right. However, some decisions go further than this on motions to strike out unfair prejudice petitions. These would bar a petitioning minority shareholder from complaining about unfair prejudice if no attempt has been made to use

---

[75] [1990] BCLC 342. The Court of Appeal also held that the discretion of the trial judge exercised under section 125(2) could be reviewed by the Court of Appeal not only on the ground of principle but on the ground of whether the petitioner had acted reasonably.

[76] [1990] BCLC 342 at 350. Balcombe LJ referred in particular to *Re Bird Precision Bellows Ltd* [1984] BCLC 395.

[77] [1973] AC 360.   [78] [1990] BCLC 342 at 350.

[79] *Re RA Noble (Clothing) Ltd* [1983] BCLC 273; *Re A Company (No. 007623 of 1984)* [1986] BCLC 362; *Re A Company (No. 004377 of 1986)* [1987] BCLC 94. See further *Re A Company (No. 006834 of 1988), ex parte Kremer* [1989] BCLC 365; where such a petition was struck out on this basis. See likewise, *Re Castleburn Ltd* [1991] BCLC 49. But cf *Re A Company (No. 005134 of 1986), ex parte Harries* [1989] BCLC 383 at 398.

the machinery provided by the articles for determining the fair value of the party's shares.[80] In view of the Court of Appeal's observations in *Virdi* v. *Abbey Leisure*,[81] these decisions would appear to be open to question where the provision in the articles allows only for a discounted minority holding basis of valuation if, under a successful section 459 petition, a *pro rata* basis would be appropriate. The observations of the Court of Appeal are applicable to unfair prejudice petitions even though the case itself concerned a just and equitable winding up.[82]

This process has been taken a stage further by Lord Hoffmann in *O'Neill* v. *Phillips*.[83] He took the opportunity to clarify the law and practice on the offer to buy as a bar to an unfair prejudice petition. This is perhaps the most useful as well as innovative aspect of the House of Lords judgment in *O'Neill*. Lord Hoffmann noted that this issue was *obiter* in that it did not arise for decision on the facts of the case. 'Nonetheless, the effect of an offer to buy the shares as an answer to a petition under section 459 is a matter of such great practical importance that I invite your Lordships to consider it.'[84]

The point of the list of criteria set out under five headings is to establish that a reasonable offer has been made so that the exclusion of the petitioner from the business of the company will not be treated as unfairly prejudicial. The petition will be struck out.

1. The offer must price the shares at a fair value. As in the existing case law, this will normally be on a *pro rata* basis, though there may be cases in which it will be fair to take a discounted value.
2. If not agreed, the value must be determined by a competent expert (e.g. an accountant agreed by the parties).
3. The offer should be to have the value determined by the expert as an expert (not full arbitration nor the halfway house of an expert who gives reasons). The objective is economy and expedition.

---

[80] See Hoffmann J in *Re A Company (No. 004377 of 1986)* [1987] BCLC 94 at 102, cited by the same judge in *Re A Company (No. 006834 of 1988), ex parte Kremer* [1989] BCLC 365 at 368. Admittedly, this is qualified in respect of cases of 'bad faith' or plain impropriety or where the articles provide for some arbitrary or artificial method of valuation.

[81] [1990] BCLC 342.

[82] See *Re A Company (No. 005134 of 1986), ex parte Harries* [1989] BCLC 383 at 398 *per* Peter Gibson J, who anticipated the Court of Appeal in *Virdi* v. *Abbey Leisure* [1990] BCLC 342. See also *Re A Company (No. 000330 of 1991), ex parte Holden* [1991] BCLC 597. In *Re Vocam Europe Ltd* [1998] BCC 396, the Court stayed a section 459 petition on the basis of an arbitration clause in an agreement between the parties.

[83] [1999] 2 BCLC 1.

[84] [1999] 2 BCLC 1 at 15. A failure to make a reasonable offer may exacerbate the unfairness alleged: *Richards* v. *Lundy* [2000] 1 BCLC 376.

4. Both parties should have the same access to information about the company relating to the value of the shares, and should have the right to make submissions to the expert.

5. Normally the offer should cover the costs of the petitioner, but the respondent should be allowed a reasonable opportunity to make an offer before being obliged to pay costs.

Lord Hoffmann, like other members of the judiciary involved in section 459 petitions, has long been aware of the dangers of the destructive effect of costs where such petitions are unnecessarily pursued. It is therefore very important that participants in such companies should be allowed to know what counts as a reasonable offer.[85] This has done much to settle and clarify an area of law and practice. It may well prove to be the aspect of O'Neill of most lasting importance to the practitioner.

The remedies available to the court

The core provisions as to remedies in section 461 are inherited from the old section 210 of the Companies Act 1948. They are in practice the most frequently employed. There is a wide power given to the court to 'make such orders as it thinks fit for giving relief in respect of the matters complained of',[86] and the most used power is to order that the complainant's shares be bought by the company (with a consequent reduction of capital) or by the majority from the minority (or vice versa).[87] There are also powers to regulate the company's affairs in the future[88] and to alter the articles and memorandum.[89]

On the recommendation of the Jenkins Committee,[90] two new powers were added (originally in 1980). These are, first, the power to order the company to refrain from doing or continuing an act complained of by the petitioner, or to do an act which the petitioner has complained it omitted to do. The second power added was to authorise civil litigation on behalf

---

[85] [1999] 2 BCLC 1 at 16. See *North Holdings Ltd* v. *South Tropics Ltd* [1999] 2 BCLC 625; [1999] BCC 746 (CA), where Morritt LJ emphasised the need for active case management at an early stage in order to reduce the time and expense involved in ascertaining a fair price for the petitioner's shares. This was the first appeal concerning section 459 proceedings under the Civil Procedure Rules 1998. See further *Re Rotadata Ltd* [2000] 1 BCLC 122. Where the petitioner and the respondent were both making offers for each other's equal holding of the company's shares, the court allowed the respondent to succeed because he had made the more reasonable offer. The respondent had adequate funds available but the petitioner lacked funds and made a vague offer lacking in vital details: *West* v. *Blanchet* [2000] 1 BCLC 795 at 803.

[86] Section 461(1). This power is 'without prejudice' to the more specific powers in section 461(2).

[87] Section 461(2)(d).   [88] Section 461(2)(g).   [89] Section 461(3).

[90] *Report of the Company Law Committee* (Cmnd 1749, HMSO, London, 1962), para. 212.

of the company 'by such person or persons and on such terms as the court may direct'.[91]

It is not surprising that in the overwhelming majority of successful petitions the 'buy-out' remedy is used, and this takes the form of the purchase by the majority of the minority's shares.[92] This remedial solution is usually the most appropriate in the disputes in small private companies on which the unfair prejudice remedy is sought. The courts have had to tackle the question of the legal basis on which the minority's shares should be valued. There is no rigid rule that in a small private company the price of a minority holding should be fixed on a *pro rata* basis or, alternatively, that the price should be discounted to reflect the fact that the shares were a minority holding. The Court of Appeal has emphasised that the overriding consideration is that the valuation is fair and equitable as between the parties. The specific power in section 461(2)(d) to order purchase is subject to the wide discretion in section 461(1) to make such order as it thinks fit for giving relief in respect of the matters complained of.[93] In practice, the *pro rata* basis will be employed where the shares have been acquired on the incorporation of a quasi-partnership and it was expected the minority shareholders would participate in the conduct of the affairs of the company. The valuation will be on the discounted basis in such a company where, in an exceptional case, the minority had acted so as to deserve exclusion. The valuation is naturally on a discounted basis where the shares are allotted or later acquired as an investment.[94]

The date of valuation of the shares is also governed by the same overriding requirement that the price should be fair. Various dates have been chosen in the light of this overriding principle.[95] The petitioner's own conduct, though not precluding a finding of unfair prejudice in his or her favour, may affect the date of valuation chosen by the court in exercising its discretion.[96]

---

[91] Section 461(2)(b) and (c).

[92] In exceptional cases, the court may order the majority to buy the minority's shares: *Re Brenfield Squash Racquets Club Ltd* [1996] 2 BCLC 184.

[93] *Re Bird Precision Bellows Ltd* [1986] 2 WLR 158 (CA). See further *Brownlow* v. *GH Marshall Ltd* [2000] 2 BCLC 655. See as to valuation under a provision in the articles, in the absence of a finding of unfair prejudice, *Re Benfield Greig Group plc* [2000] 2 BCLC 488.

[94] See Nourse J in *Re Bird Precision Bellows Ltd* [1984] Ch 419, confirmed by the Court of Appeal: [1986] 2 WLR 158. As to the appropriate method of valuation (as opposed to legal basis), see *Re Planet Organic Ltd* [2000] 2 BCLC 366.

[95] E.g. the date of the unfair prejudice, the date of the petition, or the date when the valuation is made. See further *Profinance Trust SA* v. *Gladstone* [2000] 2 BCLC 516.

[96] *Re London School of Electronics* [1986] Ch 211. Here, Nourse J considered a choice between the date of presentation of the petition and the date of valuation. Fairness may sometimes require that the shares be valued at a date earlier than the petition: *Re OC Transport Services Ltd* [1984] BCLC 251.

Note has already been taken of the court's power under section 462(2)(b) to issue what amounts to a statutory form of mandatory or prohibitory injunction.[97] The power to allow civil proceedings in the name of the company under section 461(2)(c) has not yet been much invoked. However, in one case which went to the Court of Appeal, the court appointed a receiver and manager, permitted civil proceedings in the name of the company against certain of its creditors and ordered a cancellation of an issue of shares.[98] In a Scottish case,[99] the court interdicted the holding of a meeting because the resolution to be passed would have removed a managing director from a committee responsible for company litigation. The effect of the resolution would be to put the litigation under the control of the defendants.

The use of the court's power to authorise civil proceedings in the company's name has never reached its full potential. Its use as a substitute for a derivative action in cases of corporate abuse will it is hoped be rendered largely redundant by the statutory reform of the derivative action, and possibly by the recent reform of civil procedure.

Questions remain to be answered about such consequential civil proceedings.[100] Perhaps the most important potential development in any unfair prejudice proceeding is the possibility of using a conditional fee agreement where the petitioner seeks a monetary judgment (the buy-out price of his or her shares). Although this seems not yet to have been invoked, there would seem to be no legal obstacle.[101] Indeed, there is even less difficulty than in the case of a derivative action.[102]

Procedure

As with other civil proceedings, before a full hearing of an unfair prejudice petition, the respondent may move to strike out the petition on the basis that the allegations in the petition disclose no case to answer. The judge will grant the motion to strike out if satisfied that the motion

---

[97] See p. 102 above.

[98] *Re Cyplon Developments*, unreported, Court of Appeal, 3 March 1982 (Lexis transcript).

[99] *Re Whyte* 1984 SLT 330. As to the appointment of a receiver to protect the petitioner's interests, see *Wilton Davies* v. *Kirk* [1998] 1 BCLC 214. The court's general powers to give relief under section 461(1) has been used to authorise proceedings on behalf of the company: *Re A Company (No. 005278 of 1985)* [1986] 1 WLR 281.

[100] E.g. is pro-rata recovery possible in appropriate cases and may the court grant a *Waller-steiner* order for this second stage of the proceedings?

[101] See *The Ethics of Conditional Fee Arrangements* (Society of Advanced Legal Studies, January 2001).

[102] See Chapter 2, p. 37 above.

is unarguable.[103] The Court of Appeal has held[104] that, where there has not been any finding of fact as to whether the respondents have misused any of the company's assets, it was proper for the purpose of determining whether the petition should be struck out to assume that the pleaded allegations would be established at a full hearing. The court observed that the then new Civil Procedure Rules 1998 represented a new way to conduct civil litigation that avoids the stark choice between striking out a petition and the uncertainty and expense of a full hearing.[105] The court indicated that the number of cases on which applications to strike out were made would be substantially reduced, as the parties would realise that in most cases the court-imposed directions will result in a procedure which would be so quick and cheap as to make it unwise to insert a legal step which might not succeed. Even if it did, it would not save much expense. The court was referring to the power to require a joint expert or the appointment of an assessor.

The Court of Appeal has held that a petition should be struck out where the petitioner's conduct amounted to an abuse of the process of the court. Fraudulent conduct, including destruction of documents and the production of forged documents in the discovery process, meant that it was in the interests of justice to terminate the proceedings.[106]

Chapter 5 will consider the Law Commission's proposals to reform the unfair prejudice remedy.

Access and locus standi

In the case law following the introduction of the recast unfair prejudice remedy in 1980,[107] there was some consideration of how far the 'member qua member' test of *locus standi* (imposed under section 210 of the Companies Act 1948) still applied.[108] In the case of small quasi-partnership type companies, it was soon abandoned on the basis that in such companies the 'interests of members' (referred to in what is now section 459)

---

[103] Compare *Re Legal Costs Negotiators Ltd* [1999] 2 BCLC 171 (CA), where the test was satisfied, and *Re Baltic Real Estate Ltd (No. 1)* [1993] BCLC 498, where it was not.

[104] Compare *North Holdings Ltd* v. *Southern Tropics Ltd* [1999] 2 BCLC 625 at 637.

[105] *Ibid.* at 638 *per* Aldous LJ. See likewise Morritt LJ at 639. See also *Re Rotadata Ltd* [2000] 1 BCLC 122. See further *Practice Direction (Applications Made Under the Companies Act 1985 and the Insurance Companies Act 1982)* [1999] BCC 741 *per* Sir Richard Scott. This Practice Direction is supplemental to the Civil Procedure Rules 1998, Part 49; it applies to petitions under section 459.

[106] *Arrow Nominees Inc.* v. *Blackledge* [2000] 2 BCLC 167 at 193–4 (CA).

[107] See Companies Act 1980, section 75.

[108] See Lord Grantchester QC in *Re A Company (No. 004475 of 1982)* [1983] Ch 178 at 189.

allowed the same approach to be taken as in *Ebrahimi* v. *Westbourne Galleries*.[109] It is obvious that in a small private company it is legalistic to segregate the separate capacities of the individual as shareholder, director or employee. His or her dismissal from the board or from employment by the company will inevitably affect the real value of his or her interests in the company expressed by shareholding.[110]

The distinction between enforcing 'general' company law, as opposed to the more personalised interests protected in quasi-partnership type companies, has in more recent times been conceptualised in terms of 'legitimate expectations' arising by reason of mutual confidence in such companies.[111] In a more substantial company, the concept of 'legitimate expectations' has no place.[112]

It is obvious that 'legitimate expectations' have no application in the case of a listed plc. Jonathan Parker J has observed that its introduction in the context of a listed company would 'in all probability prove a recipe for chaos. If the market in a company's shares is to have any credibility, members of the company dealing in that market must be entitled to proceed on the footing that the constitution of the company is as it appears in the company's public documents, unaffected by extraneous equitable considerations and constraints.'[113] He specifically rejected the idea that minority shareholders in such companies could have expectations based on the Listing Rules, the City Code or the Cadbury Code.[114]

The Court of Appeal has emphasised that, in general, members have no legitimate expectations beyond the legal rights conferred upon them by the constitution[115] (under general company law). This general proposition applies unless it can be shown that a 'legitimate expectation' arises out of a fundamental understanding between shareholders which formed the basis of their association. This may confer a right to participate in management.[116]

In *O'Neill* v. *Phillips*,[117] Lord Hoffmann cast some doubt on the significance of the concept of 'legitimate expectations'. Lord Hoffmann, as he readily concedes, was the 'author' of this term in respect of exclusion

---

[109] [1972] AC 360.
[110] This passage was first cited in unfair prejudice proceedings in *Re A Company (No. 004475 of 1982)* [1983] Ch 178.
[111] See e.g. *Re Kenyon Swansea Ltd* [1987] BCLC 514.
[112] *Re Postgate & Denby (Agencies) Ltd* [1987] BCLC 8; *Re Blue Arrow plc* [1987] 2 BCLC 585.
[113] *Re Astec (BSR) plc* [1998] 2 BCLC 556 at 589.   [114] *Ibid.* at 590.
[115] *Re Saul D Harrison & Sons plc* [1995] BCLC 14 at 19–20.
[116] See *R&A Electrical* v. *Haden Bill Electrical Ltd* [1995] 2 BCLC 280; *Re Regional Airports Ltd* [1999] 2 BCLC 30.
[117] [1999] 2 BCLC 1.

from management in a 'partnership type' private company.[118] In *O'Neill*, Lord Hoffmann insisted that this term, taken from public law, was only a 'label' to be attached to a conclusion that unfair prejudice had been established. 'The concept of a legitimate expectation should not be allowed to lead a life of its own capable of giving rise to equitable restraints in circumstances to which the traditional principles have no application.'[119]

Whether a 'label' or 'concept', it would seem likely that 'legitimate expectation' in the hands of the judiciary generally will remain a well-understood signpost to the equitable considerations that allow a much greater degree of judicial intervention. There is no reference in section 459 to 'minority' shareholders or members even if the unfair prejudice petition is properly regarded as a minority shareholder remedy. However, this may include a passive majority where for some reason (e.g. restructured voting rights) they are unable to take control of the board and bring company proceedings.[120]

The unfair prejudice remedy is not always confined to members currently on the register. Section 459(2) allows those to whom shares have been transferred or transmitted by operation of law (e.g. trustees in bankruptcy and personal representatives) to petition. Section 460 gives such a right to the Secretary of State for Trade and Industry (after his powers of investigation have been used), but this has been almost totally ignored by the Department of Trade and Industry.[121] As regards the normal case of petitions brought by members, this right does not extend to those with only an equitable interest in shares.[122] Likewise those who are in no sense members cannot bring a petition.[123]

Theorising 'unfair prejudice'

In the periodical literature of the last decade or so, some corporate law scholars have applied 'contractarian' theory to the unfair prejudice remedy. Before examining the work of in particular Christopher Riley[124] and Robert Goddard[125] on the application of this theory to the unfair

---

[118] See *Re A Company* (1986) 2 BCC 99, 171.   [119] [1999] 2 BCLC 1 at 11.
[120] See *Re Baltic Real Estate Ltd (No. 1)* [1993] BCLC 499; and *Re Baltic Real Estate Ltd (No. 2)* [1993] BCLC 503.
[121] See *Gore-Browne on Companies*, para. 28.26.
[122] *Re A Company (No. 007838)* (1986) BCC 98, 952.
[123] *Re A Company* [1986] BCLC 391.
[124] 'Contracting Out of Company Law: Section 459 of the Companies Act 1985 and the Role of the Courts' (1992) 55 *Modern Law Review* 782.
[125] Robert Goddard, 'Enforcing the Hypothetical Bargain: Sections 459–461 of the Companies Act 1985' (1999) 20 *Company Lawyer* 66.

prejudice remedy, some brief reference must be made to law and economics theory as it applies to company law in general. This theory has been applied to many branches of law, including tort, contract and, above all, commercial law. This intellectual movement has been very influential in the United States,[126] but also has a number of adherents in the UK.[127] It will be seen that law and economics theorists have provided a distinct analysis of company law as viewed from the perspective of this type of economic theory. Inevitably, this 'movement' has its critics among other corporate theorists, including economists.[128] Some critics object to the theory as 'anti-regulatory bias', but its adherents reject this charge. They maintain that the aim of their work is to encourage a better quality of legislative intervention based on sound economic theory.[129]

It is not appropriate in a study which does not claim to be influenced by law and economics theory to engage in detailed discussion of the assumptions made and the concepts employed by this theory,[130] except insofar as they have a particular bearing upon company law. One key idea advanced by this type of economic analysis is to stress the contractual basis of company law. In economic terms, the company is analysed as a 'network of contracts'. This essentially means that all the relationships within any particular company are best described in terms of a network of explicit or implicit bargains. This way of characterising the company is obviously at odds with the legal conception of the company[131] which centres on the legal personality of the registered company. Nevertheless, it is argued that, from an economic standpoint, thinking about the company as a nexus of contracts is an illuminating analytical exercise. The key participants – shareholders, directors and employees – can be said to become involved with their company on a voluntary basis, and to continue to interact on the basis of reciprocal expectations and behaviour. A linked

---

[126] See R. A. Posner, *Economic Analysis of Law* (Little Brown & Co., Boston, 1992); and F. L. Easterbrook and D. R. Fischel, *The Economic Structure of Corporate Law* (Harvard University Press, Cambridge, MA, 1991).

[127] E.g. A. I. Ogus, *Regulation, Legal Reforms and Economic Theory* (Oxford University Press, Oxford, 1994); and Brian Cheffins, *Company Law: Theory Structure and Operation* (Clarendon Press, Oxford, 1997).

[128] See generally McCahery, Picciotto and Scott (eds.), *Changing Structures and Dynamics of Regulation* (Clarendon Press, Oxford, 1993). See further C. A. E. Goodhart, 'Economics and Law – Too Much One Way Traffic' (1997) 60 *Modern Law Review* 1.

[129] See Brian Cheffins, *Company Law: Theory Structure and Operation* (Clarendon Press, Oxford, 1997), p. 7.

[130] See generally *ibid.*, Chapter 1, 'Economics and the Study of Company Law' for an excellent introduction to the subject.

[131] See the standard company law texts as to the concept of legal personality and the consequences of incorporation.

theory is that of the 'role of the firm'.[132] Here again, the term 'firm' does not have its usual legal meaning. Theorising about the economic utility of the 'firm' applies to enterprises which may adopt various legal forms (e.g. a partnership, a private or public limited company, or even a sole proprietor with a number of employees). In the light of such economic 'realism', it has been observed that 'company legislation has had, in and of itself, only a modest impact on the bargaining dynamics which account for the nature and form of business enterprises. Thus, analytically, an incorporated company is, like other types of firms, fundamentally a nexus of contracts.'[133]

Another theory applied by law and economics theory to the company (or any substantial enterprise) is that of 'agency costs'. Here, yet again, the term 'agency' (or the correlative 'principal') is not used in a legal sense. The theory of 'agency costs' is designed to deal with inevitable conflicts of interest between the various participants in a business enterprise. From an economic perspective, an agency relationship arises when one participant depends on another for business activity. This obviously applies to the trust that shareholders must place in company directors or officers who manage the assets and undertake the business activity of their company. This delegation by the 'principal' of the power to manage to the 'agent' raises the problem of 'agency costs'. This means the costs of monitoring the performance of the management to prevent an 'agent' from putting his own interests above those of his 'principal'. Here again, a bargaining process should establish legal arrangements that will seek to reduce agency 'costs' both in terms of the costs of continuing monitoring and the costs caused by misbehaviour or incompetent management.

Goddard,[134] following Boros,[135] pushes contractarian analysis of unfair prejudice to its full extent. This entails a distinction between two versions of the 'hypothetical bargain' model on which company law as a whole may be theorised. A distinction is made between the generalised hypothetical bargain (a highly generalised bargain based on universal expectations of participating shareholders) and the particularised hypothetical bargain. This latter involves enforcing particularised judicial examination of the structure of intra-corporate bargaining in a particular company.

---

[132] See R. H. Coase, *The Firm, the Market and the Law* (University of Chicago Press, Chicago, 1988).

[133] Brian Cheffins, *Company Law: Theory Structure and Operation* (Clarendon Press, Oxford, 1997), p. 41.

[134] Robert Goddard, 'Enforcing the Hypothetical Bargain: Sections 459–461 of the Companies Act 1985' (1999) 20 *Company Lawyer* 66.

[135] E. J. Boros, *Minority Shareholders' Remedies* (Clarendon Press, Oxford, 1995), Part II.

This is most likely to be a small private 'partnership' company where actual bargaining is likely to occur. The generalised hypothetical bargain theory accords with corporate 'common law' as well as with statutory shareholders' rights. Thus it fits in well with enforcing shareholder rights under the articles or class rights conferred in the memorandum or articles (further reinforced by statute). It would also reflect rights created by shareholders' agreements. However, Goddard[136] as well as Riley[137] also apply this contractarian analysis to the enforcement of fiduciary duties by the unfair prejudice remedy (and by implication by other common law shareholder remedies). Directors' duties can thus be regarded as implied terms enjoying the same authority as express terms, and as such their enforcement should be no different from express terms. Following this theoretical model, if contractual completeness were possible (and desirable), then common law directorial duties would be superfluous: they can, therefore, be regarded as 'an alternative to elaborate promises and extra cost monitoring'.[138]

The objections to this analysis of the whole array of varying directors' duties are obvious. The tougher and more demanding duties (in respect of good faith, proper purpose and the preservation of corporate assets) surely cannot be 'contracted away'. This is also the case in respect of the duty of care and skill. It would seem very unlikely that a minority shareholder would wish to bargain away such protections. On the other hand, the majority of shareholders might well wish to be free of the burden imposed by directors' duties to the extent they are enforceable in unfair prejudice proceedings or by other minority shareholder proceedings.

Some play, in terms of contractarian theory, is made of the nature of relief available under section 459 for mismanagement, as evidenced in cases like Re Elgindata[139] and Re Macro (Ipswich) Ltd.[140] The courts[141] have, of course, recently recognised a more demanding and objective standard of care and skill owed to the company for the purposes of other civil proceedings. It is difficult to see how these differing standards of care fit into the hypothetical bargains. It is easier to understand this dual approach in terms of self-imposed restraint upon judicial intervention in the context of unfair prejudice petitions by minority shareholders.

---

[136] Robert Goddard, 'Enforcing the Hypothetical Bargain: Sections 459–461 of the Companies Act 1985' (1999) 20 Company Lawyer 66 at 74–5.

[137] Ibid., p. 795.

[138] Goddard here cites F. L. Easterbrook and D. R. Fischel, The Economic Structure of Corporate Law (Harvard University Press, Cambridge, MA, 1991), p. 90.

[139] [1991] BCLC 959. See p. 101 above.   [140] [1994] 2 BCLC 354.

[141] See e.g. Norman v. Theodore Goddard [1991] BCLC 1028; Re D'Jan of London Ltd [1994] 1 BCLC 561.

Lord Hoffmann's recognition in *O'Neill* v. *Phillips*[142] of equitable principles as well as contractual rights or informal agreements is relevant here. It is such equitable principles that are mainly deployed to buttress judicial intervention on the ground of mutual trust and 'legitimate expectations'. Here, as was seen above,[143] there are equitable considerations that make it unfair for those conducting the affairs of the company to rely on their strict legal powers. In such 'quasi-partnership' companies, Goddard[144] applies the 'particularised hypothetical bargain' to theorise this area of application of the concept of unfair prejudice. The particularised bargain involves personal expectations rather than the universal expectations of the highly generalised hypothetical bargain.

Enforcing personal expectations requires a highly particularised examination of the structure of intra-corporate bargaining, thereby determining the basis upon which the company was formed, and those rights and expectations subsisting outside the corporate contract.[145]

Goddard applies this reasoning to a number of situations where relief has been granted by the courts in the type of company where such personal expectations can arise. In doing so, he seeks to demonstrate that Riley is wrong to find problems in applying contractarian theories. The situations considered are: exclusion or expulsion from management (as illustrated by *Westbourne Galleries*); the persistent denial of any share of the profits by way of dividend or any adequate dividend;[146] and preserving the *status quo* in a quasi-partnership company by restraining (or allowing a buy-out of shares) in the case of a prejudicial new share issue.[147]

Goddard explains his difference of approach compared to that of Riley on the grounds that Riley does not consider whether a 'non-idealised' (or real world) bargain is being considered and further as regards not distinguishing between the generalised and particularised bargains.[148] This conflict of theoretical analysis is also applied to the court's refusal in appropriate circumstances to value the shares in a buy-out in accordance with the normal practice in respect of pre-emption provisions in the

---

[142] [1999] 2 BCLC 1 at 8–11.   [143] See p. 97 above.

[144] Robert Goddard, 'Enforcing the Hypothetical Bargain: Sections 459–461 of the Companies Act 1985' (1999) 20 *Company Lawyer* 66 at 75–7.

[145] *Ibid.*, p. 70.

[146] See *Re Sam Weller & Sons Ltd* [1990] BCLC 80; and *Re A Company (No. 00370 of 1987), ex parte Glossop* [1988] 1 WLR 1068. See further p. 101 above.

[147] See *Re Cumana* [1986] BCLC 430; *Re A Company (No. 005134 of 1986), ex parte Harries* [1989] BCLC 383.

[148] Robert Goddard, 'Enforcing the Hypothetical Bargain: Sections 459–461 of the Companies Act 1985' (1999) 20 *Company Lawyer* 66 at 76. The similar views of Brian Cheffins, *Company Law: Theory Structure and Operation* (Clarendon Press, Oxford, 1997), p. 331 are likewise condemned.

company's articles. The more generous basis available to the petitioner in a successful unfair prejudice petition (i.e. *pro rata* rather than discounted as a minority holding) may apply.[149]

Ryan has several pertinent observations to make in applying the hypothetical bargain 'construct' to the legitimate expectation cases.

It must be acknowledged, however, that the courts rarely use the language of implied terms in justifying a finding of legitimate expectations. They talk rather vaguely of expectations and understandings without articulating their theoretical basis.[150]

He adds that there may be a number of areas where the courts do seem to be implying interests in the way in which a contractual model would suggest. He then observes:[151]

Some of the members' interests which the courts seem prepared to imply are so general, and so based on ordinary ideas of fairness, as to be hardly susceptible to contractual exclusion in advance. Given this, it is worth considering the extent to which the judiciary's findings of members' interests might truly be described as hypothetical bargaining, or whether the label simply disguises the judicial paradigm.

Ryan concedes[152] that the courts are developing a paradigm constitution for the class of company they are concerned with (e.g. listed, or large private or quasi-partnerships). However, the courts pay no real attention to the particular shareholders involved as opposed to hypothetical reasonable minority shareholders. There is also the problem of why, in a private company, a coherent majority bargaining *ex ante* would have conceded interests (beyond the formal contract in the articles) that the courts have implied for the minority's benefit.

In general terms it would seem that the case is well made by Ryan:[153] section 459 of the Companies Act 1985 is not merely a default provision (i.e. a provision implied in the shareholder bargain yet capable of being validly excluded). The sounder view of the unfair prejudice remedy is that it is a mandatory non-excludable provision. It provides the judges with a mechanism for *ex post facto* control of the inter-shareholder bargain. For whatever the judicial pretence that the courts merely fill gaps in the parties' agreement and will not overrule their express provisions, the

---

[149] See *Virdi* v. *Abbey Leisure* [1990] BCC 32 (CA); and *Re A Company (No. 000330 of 1991), ex parte Holden* [1991] BCLC 597. See further p. 105 above. There is also a difference of approach to the cases on the right of exit for entrapped minority shareholders. However, this 'no fault divorce' has been condemned by Lord Hoffmann in *O'Neill* v. *Phillips* [1999] 2 BCLC 1 at 13–14.

[150] (1992) 55 *Modern Law Review* 782 at 795.

[151] *Ibid.*, p. 796.　　[152] *Ibid.*, p. 797.　　[153] *Ibid.*

reality is that some terms are implied not merely to fill gaps but rather to control the operation of the parties' express terms.[154]

A comparison can be made to terms implied by law in the common law of contracts (or in the doctrine of frustration). The artificiality of basing such judge-made law on what the parties would have agreed (had they bargained *ex ante*) has long been recognised.

---

[154] *Ibid.* A notable example of these are the cases on pre-emption rights and the valuation of shares. Likewise, the power under the articles and statute (section 303 of the Companies Act 1989) to remove a director is simply ignored in the expulsion cases.

5   Reforming the statutory remedies

In this chapter the work of the Law Commission in respect of reforming the unfair prejudice remedy provided by sections 459–461 of the Companies Act 1985 (with some consequential change to just and equitable winding up under section 122(1)(g) of the Insolvency Act 1986) is explored. The work of the Department of Trade and Industry in its 1998 Consultation Paper is reviewed together with *Developing the Framework* etc. later recently published by the Company Law Review Steering Group.

The new additional unfair prejudice remedy for smaller companies

The Law Commission's Consultation Paper on shareholder remedies[1] put forward a 'suggested scheme for a new remedy for smaller companies'.[2] In its basic essentials it would apply to a private company which has a minimum of two and a maximum of five shareholders between whom there was the kind of mutual trust and participation envisaged by Lord Wilberforce in the House of Lords *Ebrahimi* v. *Westbourne Galleries*.[3]

Without the usual burden in a section 459 petition of establishing unfair prejudice, the petitioner in the envisaged procedure could apply to the court for an order on the grounds of exclusion from participation in management (or removal as a director). The petitioner would be entitled to such an order unless the respondent could establish gross misconduct on the petitioner's part. In this proposed procedure the remedy available is restricted to an order for the purchase of the petitioner's shares by other members or by the company itself. However, the purchase will

---

[1] See Law Commission, *Shareholder Remedies: A Consultation Paper* (Law Commission Consultation Paper No. 142, Stationery Office, 1996), Part 18, p. 180 (hereinafter the 'Consultation Paper').

[2] *Ibid.*, para. 18.4.

[3] [1973] AC 360 at 379. I.e. an association formed or continued on the basis of a personal relationship involving mutual confidence and an agreement or understanding that all or some of the shareholders should participate in the conduct of the business.

be at a fair value without a discount on the ground that the applicants' shares represent a minority holding.[4] In existing proceedings under sections 459–461, this is known as the distinction between a *pro rata* and a 'discounted' valuation of the minority holding.

The Law Commission was led to formulate these proposals by its own study of a number of typical section 459 petitions. It reviewed 156 petitions lodged in 1994 and 1995 in the High Court in London.[5] Of these, 96 per cent related to private companies, just under 85 per cent of which had five or fewer shareholders. Some 67 per cent of these petitions contained allegations of exclusion from management. This was by far the most commonly pleaded allegation. This study also demonstrated that in almost 70 per cent of cases the remedy sought was the purchase of the petitioner's shares.[6] The Consultation Paper emphasises that the 'new additional unfair prejudice remedy' is a reflection of these statistics.[7] The Law Commission pointed out that the most common ground on which petitioners under section 459 sought a non-discounted valuation was that the relationship between the members fell within the type contemplated in *Ebrahimi*.[8] Such a remedy would be both a 'fair result' and reduce the number of contested issues in what was designed to be a less expensive and simplified procedure.

The Law Commission's critique of its own proposals

Somewhat surprisingly, before setting out what appears to be a carefully crafted new remedy in its Consultation Paper, in that very same document the Commission not only expressed 'no provisional view as to the introduction of the new remedy', but a number of carefully weighed 'criticisms' of its own proposal.[9] These criticisms relate to various elements included in, and excluded from, the proposed remedy. The first criticism is the limit in the proposed remedy. 'It is arbitrary and it could be said that the remedy should just as well be available to companies of six shareholders, or more shares could be issued to take the company out of the scope of the remedy.' Other aspects of the new remedy (e.g. the meaning of the wording taken from *Ebrahimi* and what is meant by removal for gross misconduct) would give rise to 'extra litigation rather than settlement out of court'.[10]

---

4 See Consultation Paper, paras. 18.4–18.8.   5 Consultation Paper, para. 18.6.
6 In nearly 21 per cent it was an order for the sale of the respondent's shares.
7 As to those statistics, see Consultation Paper, Appendix E.
8 See footnote 3 above.   9 See Consultation Paper, paras. 18.2 and 18.7–18.11.
10 See Consultation Paper, para. 18.7. It qualified this criticism by observing that any new litigation would be considerably more focused than current litigation under section 459.

A further difficulty found by the Law Commission with its own suggested procedure was in restricting relief to one type of 'fault situation' (i.e. where there had been unjustified expulsion) rather than other breaches of 'legal or equitable rights or interests'. Suggestions had also been made to the Commission by practitioners and academics that the type of remedy proposed should cover 'no fault' situations where a 'buy-out' remedy would be desirable. Examples given on the Consultation Paper were: where all the parties agreed that a certain member should leave but agreement on the terms of his or her departure could not be obtained; where there was no fault by either any members or officers but some members had acquired their shares by transmission or operation of law and wanted to dispose of them; and where a member simply wanted to cease to be involved with the company.

The Consultation Paper rejects the inclusion of these 'no fault' situations by invoking one of its own 'guiding principles'.[11] This principle is to maintain the sanctity of contract binding members and the company. 'To add statutory mechanisms in situations where there is no infringement of legal or equitable rights or interests would undermine this policy.'[12] It will be seen that for this reason the Law Commission proposed 'exit remedies' in no fault situations based on model articles which can be adopted by the company. However, the Consultation Paper concedes that a case can be made for their inclusion in the statutory remedy on the ground that new provisions in Table A are unlikely to be taken up in the short term by the companies that need them (i.e. small owner-managed companies) that may not be able to afford adequate advice as to the content of their articles.

A final criticism of its new remedy made by the Consultation Paper is that it would lead to dual applications for relief based on the existing section 459 and the new remedy. The Law Commission did not propose forcing a choice between the two remedies, but petitions for both forms of relief 'would result in a multiplicity of litigation rather than a restriction of issues as intended'.[13] The answer to this criticism, the Consultation Paper suggests, lies in the active use of case management and 'particularly in the vigorous exercise by the court of its powers to determine the order in which issues are tried'.[14]

---

[11] Set out in Consultation Paper, para. 14.1.
[12] Consultation Paper, para. 18.10.   [13] Consultation Paper, para. 18.11.
[14] Consultation Paper, para. 18.11. A further 'fault' found with the new remedy was that the issue of valuation would be better determined by an independent accountant. The Consultation Paper indicates that a court could in any event make an order to this effect: Consultation Paper, para. 18.8.

The solution in the Report

The Law Commission in its Report on shareholder remedies[15] largely adopted the various criticisms advanced in its Consultation Paper against the new unfair prejudice remedy. The fact that even the Consultation Paper had such a critical approach to its own proposal indicates, very likely, that there were divided counsels within the Commission even at that stage. The Report is emphatic in rejecting the idea of a separate remedy for small private companies, and rehearses the earlier criticisms.[16] This was not based on the views of respondents in the consultation exercise between Consultation Paper and Report. The Report notes that the respondents' views, on whether or not there should be a new unfair prejudice remedy for smaller companies (along the lines proposed), 'were almost evenly split, with just a small majority in favour'.[17]

The Law Commission stresses in particular the contradiction involved in keeping such a remedy while meeting the critics' views that it lacked flexibility. 'The ideal may be to have an extensive open textured discretion as in section 459. But if the shareholder cannot afford to pursue litigation under section 459, or if the costs involved of doing so outweigh any benefit that either party will eventually obtain from the proceedings, then, however good the remedy in theory, it is of little benefit in practice. There is clearly an argument for a "rough and ready" remedy (i.e. on the lines of the Consultation Paper) which, although not perfect, can do substantial justice between the parties.'[18] It is this need that leads the Law Commission to propose what it calls an alternative approach.

The alternative approach

This 'alternative approach' aims to avoid both the duplication and the complications of 'parallel proceedings' while retaining some necessary flexibility.[19] In essence section 459 would be amended to raise presumptions that in certain circumstances:

1. where a shareholder has been excluded from participation in the management of the company, the conduct will be presumed to be unfairly prejudicial by reason of the exclusion; and

---

[15] Law Commission, *Shareholder Remedies* (Law Commission Report No. 246, Cm 3769, Stationery Office, 1997), Part 3 (hereinafter the 'Report').

[16] See Report, paras. 3.18–3.25.

[17] See Report, para. 3.14. Clearly, a consultation exercise is not regarded as a plebiscite!

[18] Report, para. 3.23.

[19] This solution is based on a proposal put forward by two respondents, Michael Crystal QC and Simon Mortimer QC, with whom Richard Adkins QC agreed.

2. if the presumption is *not* rebutted and the court is satisfied that it ought to order a buy-out of the petitioner's shares, it should do so on a *pro rata* basis.[20]

The Law Commission contend that this approach has the advantage of providing some degree of certainty for the parties (i.e. when contemplating litigation) as to the position the court is likely to take. In this respect it would, broadly, have the same effect as the separate procedure proposed in the Consultation Paper. It should mean that cases could be dealt with more quickly when proceedings are in fact started.[21]

In framing its two presumptions the Law Commission was concerned to move away from what it called 'complex factual disputes of an historical nature'.[22] It accepts that the proceedings should not focus on the past (i.e. the whole history of the company) but rather on the immediate circumstances occasioning the need for relief. Thus the proposed presumption should be based on 'structural factors' (for example, the percentage holding of the petitioner and the fact that he was a director) rather than the expectation of the parties. This has the advantage of being readily ascertainable by reference to the current or recent state of the company's affairs.

Since the new form of relief is based only on a presumption, if a case does not satisfy the conditions for a presumption to arise, a petition under section 459 could still be pursued by showing the exclusion from management was unfairly prejudicial.[23] The Law Commission's detailed proposals refine the situation in which the proposed presumptions would operate. First, they would be confined to private companies limited by shares.[24] Secondly, the presumption would apply where the petitioner had been excluded from management. This means that he or she has been removed as a director or has been prevented from carrying on all or substantially all his or her functions as a director.[25] Thirdly, the presumption was concerned essentially with owner-managed companies. In more closely defined terms this means that the petitioner should hold not less than 10 per cent of the voting rights. These voting rights must be exercisable 'at a general meeting of the company on all or substantially all matters'. The shares must be held solely (i.e. not jointly) in the petitioner's own name.[26]

---

[20] See Report, paras. 3.27–3.30.   [21] Report, para. 3.28.
[22] Report, para. 3.35.   [23] See Report, para. 3.37.
[24] This obviously excludes unlimited companies, and companies limited by guarantee. See Report, paras. 3.38–3.39.
[25] See Report, paras. 3.40–3.43. This will not include the petitioner's spouse or someone nominated as a director by the petitioner.
[26] Report, para. 3.45–3.47.

The other requirement as to the structure of the company is that all, or substantially all, of the members are directors. This reflects the need to target owner-managed companies.[27] In determining these two elements (10 per cent shareholding and the need for substantially all the shareholders to be directors), the shares held on trust or by nominee holders are to be ignored in order to avoid undue complexity in what is designed to be a straightforward and practical solution. Thus shares not held in the petitioner's name (or the other owner-managers' names) will be ignored. However, a petitioning shareholder who wants to have the benefit of the presumption will not be prevented from creating a trust of his shares – but if he does so he must remain sole holder of shares carrying at least 10 per cent of the voting rights. As respects the shares over which he creates a trust, it will be sufficient if he or she ensures that he or she is a trustee and is the first named joint holder.[28]

These factors raising the presumptions must exist immediately before the exclusion from participation in management.[29] The presumption does not require a limit on the total number of shareholders in a company. 'This is because the requirement that all, or substantially all, of the members are directors will inevitably place a limit on the size of the companies which come within the terms of the presumption.'[30]

Practical working of the presumptions

Where the conditions described above are met, the first presumption will operate so that the affairs of the company will be presumed to have been conducted in a manner which is unfairly prejudicial for the purposes of section 459(1) unless the contrary is shown. This will mean that the onus will be on the respondent to show that the affairs of the company have *not* been conducted in a manner which is unfairly prejudicial to the petitioner. Thus it will be open to the respondent to show that the petitioner has no legitimate expectation of being able to continue to participate in the management of the company or that removal was justified because of the petitioner's conduct.[31]

It was seen that the second presumption would provide that where the first presumption has not been rebutted and the court is satisfied that it ought to make an order that one or more of the respondents should purchase the petitioner's shares, the shares should be valued on a *pro rata* basis unless the court otherwise orders.[32] It will be for the court to determine who shall buy the shares where there are a number of respondents. In some situations the second presumption may be displaced

---

[27] Report, para. 3.48.   [28] See Report, para. 3.50.   [29] See Report, para. 3.51.
[30] Report, para. 3.52.   [31] Report, paras. 3.54–3.55.   [32] Report, para. 3.62.

by the circumstances. This may be the case, for example, where the shares are preference shares with a fixed right to dividends and return of capital. The court will retain its existing wide discretion to give ancillary directions. This would include determining the date at which the shares should be valued.[33]

A further pre-trial procedure is proposed by the Law Commission in support of the operation of the second presumption (as to valuation). It is suggested that the petitioner should be required to serve notice on other members of the company (and on the company) requiring them to purchase his shares valued on a *pro rata* basis, if at the time of the proceedings he intends to rely on the second presumption. The purpose of this 'buy-out notice' is to 'encourage parties to settle disputes, or at least to set out their respective positions on the question of a buy-out, before the proceedings commenced'.[34] Failure to do so would not prevent the presumptions operating in otherwise appropriate cases, but the court should have the power to sanction the failure to comply with the notice requirement in making an appropriate costs order.[35]

'No fault' situations excluded

The Law Commission, in its Report, decided to exclude the use of its proposed procedure in 'no fault' situations. It was strongly opposed on economic grounds to allow shareholders to 'exit' at will by statutory procedure. Such a right would be fundamentally contrary to the sanctity of the contract binding the members and the company which should guide the approach to shareholders' remedies.[36] The Commission acknowledged the utility of a right of exit but regarded this as a matter for the articles of association and 'model articles'.[37]

Reflections and subsequent developments

There is much to recommend the Law Commission's proposals to meet the common case of expulsion from management in owner-managed companies. It shares with Lord Hoffmann's exegesis of the case law in *O'Neill* v. *Phillips*[38] a concern to reduce the incidence of expensive litigation in small private companies by providing a more predictable

---

[33] Report, paras. 3.60–3.61.   [34] Report, para. 3.63.
[35] This procedure, the Law Commission suggested, should form part of the pre-action protocols (within the Civil Procedure Rules 1998), and should be set out in a Practice Direction by the Vice-Chancellor: Report, para. 3.64.
[36] Report, para. 3.66. See Consultation Paper, para. 14.11.
[37] See further Report, Part 5 on articles of association, discussed at p. 133 below.
[38] [1999] 1 WLR 1092, on which see Chapter 4, p. 96 above.

procedure. This might encourage more of such claims to be settled either out of court or before a hearing. The Law Commission's 'presumptions' were derived from proposals made by some distinguished practitioners.[39] However, their solution does not appear to have received much welcome in the Department of Trade and Industry's further consultation process. In *Developing the Framework*[40] it is observed that these responses 'were mixed and inconclusive'. Some argued that the two presumptions 'would encourage litigation'. It was even argued that 'they were open to abuse because it is not in fact reasonable to assume that removal from management under the conditions suggested is inequitable'.[41]

Seemingly on the basis of these rather vague allegations, the Company Law Review Steering Group were inclined 'on balance' to doubt whether the case for the presumptions has been made.

It is also doubtful whether the presumptions are consistent with *O'Neill* v. *Phillips*.[42] This does not augur well for a constructive reform of the unfair prejudice remedy in general or for a better procedure in the case of owner-managed companies.

In *Completing the Structure*, published in November 2000, the Company Law Review Steering Group takes a harder line against any change to the existing law. It acknowledges that the views of respondents to its earlier suggestions in *Completing the Framework* as to what to do about the *O'Neill* case were very mixed.[43] Most respondents favoured removing the 'contractual' restraint in *O'Neill* and allowing any cases to be brought which raised an argument that the claimant had been unfairly prejudiced on particular facts – whether or not an agreement of some kind had been reached.

Most of the minority of respondents who favoured keeping *O'Neill* supported additional remedies in specifically defined situations (see below). Some (a minority of the minority who favoured keeping *O'Neill*) expressed concern about how such remedies were to be defined. They feared that, whether or not *O'Neill* was retained, such specific remedies might constrain the scope of the general remedy in future.

---

[39] See footnote 19 above.

[40] DTI Company Law Review Steering Group, *Modern Company Law for a Competitive Economy: Developing the Framework* (DTI, URN 00/656, March 2000), para. 4.104.

[41] *Ibid.*

[42] [1999] 1 WLR 1092. The DTI Company Law Review Steering Group, *Modern Company Law for a Competitive Economy: Completing the Structure* (DTI, URN 00/1335, November 2000), affirms this rejection of the Law Commission's proposals in a fairly dismissive manner. See *ibid.*, para. 5.76. See further DTI Company Law Review Steering Group, *Modern Company Law for a Competitive Economy: Final Report* (DTI, URN 01/942 and URN 01/943, July 2001), vol. I, para. 7.41, which confirms the rejection of the Law Commission's proposal. It also recommends against reversing *O'Neill* v. *Phillips*. It also rejects 'specific remedies'.

[43] See *ibid.*, paras. 5.77–5.79.

It is this very cautious and conservative approach that the Steering Group endorses – even though it lacks the support of most respondents. The Steering Group ignores the question of how far *O'Neill* will in practice restrain the courts in future. *O'Neill* provides much more leeway than the Steering Group's terse account of its reasoning reveals. Combined with the rejection by the Steering Group of the Law Commission's 'presumptions' in the case of expulsion in owner-managed companies, it will allow unfair prejudice petitions to foster open-ended and expensive litigation in small private companies. *O'Neill* may well prove no more than a method of 'theorising' the concept of unfair prejudice. Its remedially polymorphous character may survive the apparent 'contractual' straitjacket.[44]

The Steering Group's rejection of specific remedies (the discretion to refuse share transfers, the protection of class rights and the alteration of shareholders' property rights) may well be justified. The Steering Group maintain that the courts can give adequate protection in these areas under the existing unfair prejudice remedy. This the courts may well do uninhibited by *O'Neill* which may have little restrictive effect. To conclude, the Steering Group's rejection of the Law Commission's solution to the problem of expulsion from owner-managed companies is regrettable. This might have proved a much better brake upon the abuse of the section 459 remedy than *O'Neill* is ever likely to do.[45]

On a more positive note, *Developing the Framework*[46] is prepared to resist the narrowing effect of *O'Neill v. Phillips*. It goes so far as to suggest 'the decision in *O'Neill v. Phillips* be reversed by declaring that unfairness be regarded as arising on the facts, rather than because of some breach of agreement or some principle of equity in relation to the constitution, or on the basis of the legitimate expectation of the petitioner, or in some other way'.[47]

Taking an alternative tack, consultees are asked whether 'section 459 should be left as it is, accepting the *O'Neill* ruling', but with the addition of specific remedies for cases lying outside the principles seemingly established by the House of Lords. Reference is then made to the Law Commissioner's presumptions in favour of a member excluded from management, economic harm to class interests and unfair refusals to transfer shares. Consultees are then asked whether there are any other areas where such a specific remedy should be added or whether those cases should be dealt with by extending the definition of personal rights.[48] This range of options leaves everything very much in the air. It recognises the

---

[44] See Chapter 4, p. 98 above.   [45] See *Completing the Structure*, paras. 5.80–5.81.
[46] *Developing the Framework*, paras. 4.100–4.110. But this proposal is rejected in the Final Report (see footnote 42 above).
[47] See *ibid.*, Question 4.5(a).   [48] See *ibid.*, Question 4.5(b).

undesirable narrowing effect of *O'Neill* and the need for a wider range of situations to be embraced by section 459,[49] as well as for an expeditious remedy for small companies.

The Law Commission in its Report on shareholder remedies was not in favour of amending the existing wording of section 459 (i.e. as to the general remedy) even if this were designed to make the remedy more readily available. It is better to leave it to the courts to extend the existing remedy as they see fit.

Winding up as a section 461 remedial order

A significant change in the remedial orders that a court may make under section 461 was proposed in the Report on shareholder remedies.[50] This additional power would have advantages over the existing situation where a petition for unfair prejudice can be combined with a petition under section 122(1)(g) of the Insolvency Act 1986 seeking a winding up order on the just and equitable ground.[51] Although this may be done in the same petition, the Law Commission found that the difference between the two jurisdictions could complicate matters. It proposed to streamline shareholders' remedies, and increase the court's power to deal flexibly with shareholders' problems by amending section 461 of the Companies Act 1985 to add winding up to the existing list of remedies available to a court where unfair prejudice has been established. As a safeguard, the court's leave should be required in order to apply for this new remedy. This would also apply where a winding-up order under section 122(1)(g) of the Insolvency Act 1986 is sought in conjunction with an application under section 459 of the Companies Act 1985.

The Law Commission itself[52] recognised that a number of objections might be raised against this proposal. One factor is that winding up is very different in nature from the other remedies currently available under section 461. These latter deal with rearranging the management or capital structure of a continuing company while, very obviously, winding up is concerned with terminating the company's existence. It is true that, in the case of winding up, some shareholders may buy back the business from the liquidator and continue to run it, while in the case of a purchase

---

[49] This need *not* to 'straitjacket' section 459 petitions. This was fully recognised in the Consultation Paper, paras. 20.17–20.23.

[50] See Report, paras. 4.24–4.49. This 'reform option' was canvassed in the Consultation Paper, although no provisional recommendation was made. See Report, para. 4.24; and Consultation Paper, paras. 20.24–20.28.

[51] As to the relationship between these two remedies, see Chapter 4, p. 102 above.

[52] DTI Consultation Paper on Shareholder Remedies (DTI, URN 98/994, November 1998), para. 3.5.

order under section 461 some shareholders may leave, having sold their shares to others who continue the business in its existing corporate form. The Law Commission sought to deal with unnecessary winding up applications (whether under section 461 or section 122(1)(g)) and so discourage vexatious petitions, by recommending that the court's leave should be required before a minority shareholders' petition sought a winding up or where this was brought in conjunction with an application under section 459.

In seeking the views of respondents the DTI makes a 'general counter argument'[53] against the Law Commission's recommendation. This is that the making of a winding up order causes damage to the company's business and reputation which would be less likely to occur in the case of a share purchase order. Moreover, while in the case of a winding up order some shareholders might be able to buy the business back from the liquidator, it could be argued that they would run the risk of the liquidator selling the business to a third party who made a higher bid. The DTI also argue that adding winding up to the remedies available under section 461(2) would raise the possibility that a company could be wound up in circumstances where the 'just and equitable' test in section 122(1)(g) would not have been satisfied and where, therefore, the company could not have been wound up under that section. The DTI[54] still concedes that there are possible benefits in adding winding up to the remedies available under section 461. It would obviously remove the anomaly of having to make two applications even though in substance the court would consider a single case. There may also be cost savings. However, since this reform was only canvassed but not proposed in the Law Commission's Consultation Paper,[55] it needs to be more widely canvassed. Those consultees who did comment on the issue did not consider that the absence of winding up from the section 461 remedies caused problems in practice. In conclusion, the DTI's Consultation Paper specifically asks all its respondents to weigh the advantages and disadvantages of making a legislative change in this area.[56]

Requirements for leave

This new requirement is intended to prevent a petitioner seeking a winding up order primarily as a means of putting pressure on the other side

---

[53] See *ibid.*, paras. 4.26–4.27. See further 'Shareholder Remedies, Memorandum by the Company Law Committee' (No. 373, February 1999), para. 1 of the Committee's response to the Consultation Paper.
[54] DTI Consultation Paper on Shareholder Remedies, para. 3.17.
[55] Consultation Paper, paras. 20.24–20.28.
[56] DTI Consultation Paper on Shareholder Remedies, para. 3.8.

even though it is not the form of relief the petitioner really prefers or is not likely to obtain. In such cases, there is a real risk that a company will suffer reputational damage and loss of confidence among its suppliers and customers if an application is made unjustifiably.[57] In the leave application, the court can take these factors into account. In any event, the Law Commission stresses that winding up should remain a weapon of last resort.[58] This requirement of leave will apply to both winding up as a new remedy under section 461 and a petition for just and equitable winding up under section 122(1)(g) (when this is combined with a section 459 petition).[59]

The Law Commission proposes certain consequential amendments to the Insolvency Act 1986 to protect creditors and those dealing with the company. The most notable is that where a petition under section 459 is amended to include a claim for winding up (whether under section 122(1)(g) or under the new provision) the winding up should be deemed to commence from the date of the amendment.[60] It is also proposed that members seeking winding-up relief under section 461 (unlike petitions under section 122(1)(g)) need not have held their shares for six months. The grounds for relief under section 461 (unfair prejudice) will still remain distinct from those for a just and equitable winding up under section 122(1)(g).[61]

The consultation exercise has been carried a stage further and the results are reflected in *Developing the Framework*.[62] This indicates that the responses to the DTI Consultation Paper[63] were 'very mixed, with strong views on either side and a small majority in favour' (i.e. of adding just and equitable winding up to the forms of relief available under section 461). Those in favour of the change thought it would streamline proceedings, add flexibility and strengthen the hands of petitioners. This was qualified by the view of some (in favour) that winding up should be subject to tight control and be used only as a measure of last resort. Those consulted, whose views were against the change, argued that the threatened use of this remedy would subject companies to prolonged uncertainty, threaten unemployment and be open to abuse and pressure.

---

[57] Report, para. 4.39.   [58] Report, para. 4.41.

[59] Report, para. 4.42. The 1990 Practice Direction, *Practice Direction (Company Court: Contributors Petition)* [1990] 1 WLR 490, will be replaced. This is regarded as inadequate.

[60] See Report, paras. 4.43–4.46. This of course relates to the provisions in sections 127–129 of the Insolvency Act 1986.

[61] See Report, paras. 4.36–4.38.

[62] *Developing the Framework*, para. 4.105. This has been confirmed by the Steering Group in *Completing the Structure*, para. 5.76.

[63] DTI, URN 98/994, November 1998.

They therefore maintained that the safeguards surrounding winding up proceedings on the 'just and equitable' ground under section 122(1)(g) should be preserved.

The Company Law Review Steering Group concluded by supporting those opposed to change. 'The strongest argument against allowing the remedy under section 459, which on balance we accept, was that the ability to include a claim for such a remedy risks endangering the viability of companies.'[64]

Proposed limitation period for unfair prejudice proceedings

In its Report on shareholder remedies, the Law Commission considered the question of whether there should be a limitation period in respect of claims brought under sections 459–461 (there being none at present). It concluded that there should be such a statutory time limit, but that the length of the limitation period and 'other relevant details' should be considered in the context of the Law Commission's own current project on limitation of actions in England and Wales.[65] Although the Commission's final views are not yet known, its Consultation Paper on limitation of actions was published in January 1998.[66] In respect of section 459 proceedings, the Law Commission[67] expresses the provisional view that proceedings under section 459 should be subject to the 'core regime' proposed in their Consultation Paper. The application of this regime would mean that the shareholder would have three years to bring the application from the date when he or she knew or ought reasonably to have known of the facts constituting the allegedly unfairly prejudicial conduct. This would then be subject to a 'long stop' of ten years from the date of the incident alleged to constitute unfairly prejudicial conduct.

However, the Law Commission[68] itself recognises that its proposals might give rise to difficulties in certain cases. This is particularly so as regards the 'ten-year long stop'. It notes that, particularly in cases based on a series of incidents, it may be difficult to determine when the cause of action actually accrues or when the long stop period begins. Thus shareholders may face difficulty in obtaining the information relevant to their claim.[69]

---

[64] *Developing the Framework*, para. 4.105. This is further confirmed in the Final Report (see footnote 42 above), vol. I, para. 7.41.
[65] DTI Consultation Paper on Shareholder Remedies, para. 3.9.
[66] DTI Consultation Paper on Shareholder Remedies (DTI, URN 98/994, November 1998).
[67] *Ibid.*, paras. 13.154–13.158.   [68] *Ibid.*   [69] *Ibid.*, para. 3.10.

The Law Commission itself asked consultees a number of questions about its proposals. The DTI poses its version of these question to its respondents. Respondents are asked for their views as to whether there should be a time limit for bringing claims under section 459 and, if so, whether the Law Commission's provisional view that the 'core regime' proposed in its Consultation Paper on limitation of actions should apply. The DTI itself[70] suggest an alternative approach to imposing a statutory time limit. This is based on judicial review procedure. It would require the leave of the court to pursue an application, with or without the obligation to proceed promptly after the grounds for the application arose.[71]

Procedural changes

The Law Commission's Report concludes with some other procedural changes to hearing section 459 petitions. It is proposed that the Lord Chancellor consider changes to the Unfair Prejudice Proceedings Rules 1986[72] to give the court the procedural power to hear contribution and indemnity claims in section 459 proceedings.[73] Another change in the 1986 Rules was proposed to include an express provision stating that no advertisement of a section 459 petition should take place except in accordance with an order of the court, and to confirm the meaning given by the courts to 'advertisement' in this context by an appropriate definition.[74] A suggestion that former members be permitted to bring proceedings under section 459 was rejected.[75]

The outlook for reform

The most important forms of minority shareholders' remedy in modern company law and practice must be the twin statutory minority remedies under section 459 of the Companies Act 1985 and section 122(1)(g) of the Insolvency Act 1986. The overwhelming incidence of their use (especially section 459) is evidence enough of their significance. It should follow that this should be the most important aspect of the Law Commission's reforming work. It has been seen that the Commission eschewed

---

[70] *Ibid.*, para. 3.11.
[71] *Ibid.*, para. 3.12 also asks its respondents to give a view as to whether, for Scottish cases under section 459, there should be a prescriptive period, and, if so, whether it should be the same as the existing short negative prescription (five years) or whether there should be a specific limitation period, and, if so, what period would be appropriate.
[72] SI 1986 No. 2000.
[73] Report, paras. 4.50–4.53. See now the Civil Procedure Act 1997.
[74] Report, paras. 4.54–4.56.   [75] Report, paras. 4.57–4.60.

any attempt to make a radical restatement of these remedies. In this its judgment must surely be right. Its labours in this area, despite their significance for practitioners, has attracted much less attention from academic commentators than the statutory reform of the derivative action.[76]

In the Commission's Report, the more cautious approach (compared with its Consultation Paper) to a distinct unfair prejudice remedy for small owner-managed private companies is amply justified. Even the Consultation Paper advances powerful arguments against its 'parallel proceedings' solution. The other significant change proposed in the Report – adding winding up to the remedial orders available to the court under section 461 – appears well argued. It provides a better solution than the present duality of remedies under section 459 and section 122(1)(g).

The over-cautious views expressed in *Developing the Framework* seem to be regrettably negative and hesitant. The level of argument is rather superficial compared with that in the Law Commission's Consultation Paper and Report. It remains to be seen what more detailed 'preparatory work' will be published by the Company Law Review Steering Group before legislative policy is finally settled.

The right of exit: shareholders' self-help

The Law Commission's Report rejected the idea that its recasting of the unfair prejudice remedy should extend to 'no fault' situations where a minority shareholder desired to leave the company and wanted his or her shares purchased. This rejection was posited on the basis of the 'fourth guiding principle', sanctity of contract, set out in the introductory chapter to the Report.[77] The Law Commission elsewhere expressed its view that there are strong economic arguments against allowing shareholders to exit at will. Such a right would fundamentally contravene the sanctity of the contract binding the members and the company.[78] In both the Consultation Paper[79] and the Report,[80] it is proposed that a qualified exit right should be provided for in a reformed Table A. The policy aim is to encourage shareholders to provide in advance for what was to happen in the event of a dispute. This would help to avoid litigation in many cases or at least clear the ground by substantially reducing the issues in dispute. The proposed 'Draft Regulation 119: Exit Right'[81] is designed to give a carefully balanced method of leaving the company where a shareholder is

---

[76] See, however, John Lowry, (1997) 18 *Company Lawyer* 247 at 253–5, who criticises the Consultation Paper in respect of the 'additional unfair prejudice remedy'.
[77] See Report, para. 1.9.   [78] See Report, paras. 3.65–3.66.
[79] Consultation Paper, para. 19.2.   [80] Report, para. 5.1.
[81] See Report, Appendix C.

disaffected without the need to resort to section 459 proceedings which would involve costly and cumbersome litigation. The key qualification in Regulation 119 is that it requires an ordinary resolution before exit rights could be attached to particular shares. No particular circumstances for triggering these exit rights are set out. It is left to the company to set these out (if required) in the resolution. The rights created by the resolution would be exercised by service of notice requiring those on whom the notice is served to purchase the shares of the shareholder wishing to exit.[82]

The Report notes that there was widespread support for an exit article along the lines proposed. A few respondents had reservations. One criticism was that providing exit routes might prove economically damaging and lead to the break-up of small businesses at the first sign of disagreement. The Report rejects this argument as applied to its carefully qualified proposal. Rather than encouraging break-up, Regulation 119 is intended to encourage the parties to make provision for future breakdown in their relations so as to minimise the disruption in the company's business.[83] The Report also dismisses the argument that an exit right enables minority shareholders to exert improper pressure on the basis that the other side could not afford to pay for the shares. There is no reason to think that this will give rise to any particular difficulties beyond any other minority remedy.[84] A further critique was that the specialised and particular nature of the proposed exit right was unsuitable for inclusion in the general character of Table A. The Report responds to this argument by pointing out that it leaves it to the company to decide when the exit rights will apply.[85] 'The article is therefore very versatile and does not suffer from the difficulties to which a standard form pre-emption article would give rise.'[86]

Circumstances giving rise to exit right

In the Consultation Paper,[87] the proposed exit right in the articles was confined to companies with less than ten members. This could readily be evaded by splitting shareholdings. The Report regards the ten-member limit as unnecessary and possibly arbitrary. Since the company has to pass

---

[82] See Report, para. 5.5 and Appendix C, Draft Regulation 19(2) and 19(3). Further models of this right are discussed below.
[83] See Report, paras. 5.7–5.8.
[84] Thus pre-emption rights, common in the articles of private companies, were never included in Table A.
[85] I.e. either by passing a special resolution or by modifying Draft Regulation 119 to set out the relevant circumstances.
[86] See Report, paras. 5.6 and 5.9.   [87] See Consultation Paper, para. 19.11.

a resolution to bring the article into effect, this is a sufficient restriction on its applicability.[88]

In the Law Commission's Report, the view was taken that the remedy should be available both in situations where an unfair prejudice petition might be brought and on 'no fault' situations where a right of exit might be desired.[89] The solution adopted was not to limit the remedy but to give two examples of very common situations in which shareholders are likely to want to invoke exit rights. The two situations are: (a) the removal of a shareholder who is a director from his office as a director of the company; and (b) the death of a shareholder.[90] The company is free, in applying draft Regulation 119,[91] to specify in the resolution any specified event or events deemed desirable. The resolution must also name the shareholder or shareholders to which it applies and the latter must consent to it. The resolution must also name those shareholders required to buy the shares at a 'fair price'. The exit right must be exercised by giving notice to the company and to the named shareholders required to buy the shares.[92] To qualify, the shares must have been held when the resolution was passed.[93] The notice may not be withdrawn unless all the shareholders named in the resolution agree.[94]

The method of valuation

The resolution must state how the 'fair price' is to be calculated. Various possible methods of determining this calculation are listed for convenience.[95] It is for the company to decide which to adopt, but the resolution is invalid unless it contains a provision as to the meaning of a fair price.[96] Those methods listed are: determination by an independent person (acting as an expert valuer and not as an arbitrator or arbiter); a price representing a rateable value;[97] in the case of shares which do not carry a right to participate in a winding up, a price representing their net asset value as determined by an independent person; in the case of shares which do not carry a right to participate in surplus assets in a winding up, a price equal to the capital sum paid for them. The company must select what is regarded as the most appropriate basis. This must be stated in the resolution.

---

[88] Report, para. 5.13.   [89] Report, paras. 5.17–5.18.
[90] I.e. allowing exit to the personal representative.
[91] Report, Appendix C(3).   [92] Report, Appendix C(2).
[93] Or be shares acquired in the right of them (e.g. bonus shares).
[94] See Report, para. 5.29.
[95] Report, Appendix C, Draft Regulation 119(6).   [96] *Ibid.*
[97] See Report, Appendix C, Draft Regulation 119(7) for the formula for an independent person to determine the rateable value of shares of a particular class.

'Independent person'

The Report[98] defines the 'independent' person, who is given the task of making the valuation of the shares, as 'an independent person who appears to have the requisite knowledge and experience'. In the Consultation Paper,[99] the definition was 'an independent accountant'. The Law Commission accepted the argument that the company's auditor or another accountant may not always be the best person to value the shares. It is pointed out that share valuation requires particular skills which do not necessarily form part of an accountant's training or practice. There are experienced valuers who are not accountants. As regards the company's auditor, there may well be a conflict of interest between the interests of the exiting shareholder and the ongoing relationship of the auditor to the company.[100] The manner of appointment of the independent person is to be provided in the resolution creating the exit rights. Provision is made as to recovery of the purchase price after a valuation is made. The Report[101] rejects the Consultation Paper's suggestion that the exiting shareholders have the right to wind up the company if the remaining shareholders failed to purchase his or her shares within the timescale provided. The Report notes the difficulties such a remedy might create (e.g. if only one or two shareholders out of many failed to purchase some of the outgoing shareholders' shares). It would also allow unjustifiable pressure to be placed on those shareholders. Instead, the Report[102] concludes that the exiting shareholders could simply invoke the ordinary contractual remedy of specific performance.[103]

The Report deals with problems caused by certain changes in circumstances which will cause a resolution (creating exit rights) to cease to have effect before the shareholder can invoke the rights created. The first circumstance arises where a shareholder (named as buyer in the resolution) ceases to hold the shares which he held when the resolution was passed.[104] This is without prejudice of course to any exit notice which has already been served.[105] To prevent this provision being abused by the transfer of shares designed to destroy exit rights, draft Regulation 119 provides that directors must refuse to register a transfer which would

---

[98] See Report, para. 5.26 and Appendix C, Draft Regulation 119(13).

[99] See Report, Appendix C, Draft Regulation 119(5).

[100] Report, para. 5.26. As to the procedure applicable to the work of the independent person, see Appendix H, Draft Regulation 119(10).

[101] Report, para. 5.28; Consultation Paper at 19.8.   [102] *Ibid.*

[103] Report, para. 5.28. The Report also rejects the proposal for a provision for the payment of the purchase price by instalments: Report, para. 5.30.

[104] See Report, para. 5.23 and Appendix C, Draft Regulation 119(6). This provision can be excluded in the resolution.

[105] Report, Appendix C, Draft Regulation 119(16)(a).

cause the resolution to be ineffective.[106] The second circumstance which will cause the resolution to cease to have effect (unless the resolution states otherwise) is when a named shareholder dies. The reason for this provision is that it would delay the administration of the estate if there was potential liability to purchase the shares of other named shareholders which remained outstanding. The provision is of course without prejudice to any exit notice already served before the death. In addition, if it is the death of a shareholder which triggers the exercise of the exit right by his or her successor, the resolution is to continue so far as that event is concerned.[107]

Appraisal of the exit remedy

The 'exit' remedy as amended by the Law Commission's Report on shareholder remedies appears to be a well-thought-out and crafted 'self help' measure. It carefully balances the various opposed interests involved. It is obviously true that only many years of experience of its practical working will enable a fuller picture to be drawn of its utility, fairness and robustness. It is strange that the Company Law Review Steering Group has made adverse comment on this aspect of the Law Commission's work,[108] even though in terms of the affairs of the mass of small private companies the proposed exit remedy, if implemented in a reformed Table A, may prove much the most important change made in minority shareholders' remedies. It is far more attractive than litigation. In view of the debatable quality and clarity of the Steering Group's attempts to revise and 'improve' the Law Commission's work, it is perhaps fortunate that this omission has occurred.

Other 'additions' to Table A rejected

The Law Commission proposed in its Consultation Paper[109] a draft regulation[110] (for inclusion in Table A) providing for arbitration of disputes between shareholders and the company. This would apply to any type or size of company but would be confined to disputes that could be litigated. It also provided that the arbitration proceedings would be suspended if parties sought instead to use an alternative dispute resolution

---

[106] Report, Appendix C, Draft Regulation 119(20).
[107] Report, para. 5.24. See Report, Appendix C, Draft Regulation 119(16)(b).
[108] See *Developing the Framework* and *Completing the Framework*. See p. 139 below. The DTI's Consultation Paper on Shareholder Remedies (November 1998) 8.9 supports the exit article.
[109] Consultation Paper, para. 19.11.
[110] See Consultation Paper, Appendix H, Draft Regulation 120.

procedure (e.g. mediation).[111] The Law Commission's Report was not impressed by the need to include an arbitration article in Table A as opposed to an article which private companies might draft for themselves. Although a small majority of respondents favoured an arbitration article in Table A, the Law Commission was more impressed by the arguments of a majority of practising lawyers as to the problems that might occur.[112] Among the more persuasive of these arguments were: (a) the likely disputes as to whether the complaints of the shareholders were not an appropriate subject of legal proceedings; and (b) that the interests of other shareholders might be affected but it is not clear how they were to be represented in arbitration proceedings. It may be added that the practical utility of arbitration in the case of public companies is seriously open to question. The Law Commission[113] concluded that the difficulties of the proposal outweighed the benefits. It was of course open to the parties to shareholder/company disputes to resort to arbitration or other alternative dispute resolution procedures.

The Law Commission[114] also rejected a draft regulation proposed in its Consultation Paper[115] to provide in Table A for a valuation procedure. This was intended to meet the situation where all the shareholders in a company agree that one or more of them should sell their shares to the rest but could not agree on the price. This valuation procedure was designed to avoid an unnecessary petition under section 459. The Law Commission, however, accepted the criticisms of a number of respondents as to how such a Table A regulation could work in practice. The Law Commission were concerned that the parties should not be bound by a valuation procedure at too early a stage since this might discourage them from entering into negotiations at all. If, on the other hand, the regulation was only to apply when the parties have reached an effective agreement, this requires that they must either have agreed on the price or on a method of fixing the price. In the form proposed in the Consultation Paper,[116] the draft regulation would have had the effect of imposing a *pro rata* basis of valuation. This basis of valuation might not meet the needs or intentions of the parties as to the basis on which the third party valuer should determine the price. The arguments of the Law Commission rejecting a draft regulation on arbitration and a draft regulation on valuation

---

[111] See Consultation Paper, paras. 19.13–19.14.   [112] Report, para. 5.36.
[113] Report, para. 5.30. The DTI's Consultation Paper on Shareholder Remedies, para. 12.8 accepts the Law Commission's view.
[114] Report, paras. 5.39–5.48.
[115] Consultation Paper, paras. 19.16–19.17. See Appendix H, Draft Regulation 121.
[116] See Consultation Paper, para. 19.16 and Appendix H, Draft Regulation 121(2).

procedure (as candidates for a new Table A) seem well made and based on sound practical considerations.

The Company Law Review Steering Group takes, here again, a dismissively negative stance towards the Law Commission's proposed 'exit article'.[117] The Committee states that 'the proposed article was carefully considered in our working group on small firms and in the group on shareholders' rights'. The 'clear conclusion' reached by these groups was that the exit article would not be used in practice because on commercial grounds it would not be incorporated in company constitutions by well-informed founders and was inherently undesirable on the grounds of lack of flexibility. 'It was impossible to prescribe in advance, and for the full diversity of companies, what would be a fair exit regime. For ill-informed founders it would be a trap.'

All this ignores the fact the Law Commission received widespread support for an exit article. The reservations of a 'few respondents' were taken into account in the Law Commission's revised version of the exit article. The dismissive opinions quoted by the Steering Group would seem to require much fuller elaboration on the public record if they are to form the basis of inaction by the DTI. An exit article is not forced on a company wishing to exclude it, and when operative can only be invoked on the basis of a majority resolution. The assertions of the working groups must beg some questions since the Law Commission's article will never be tested in practice. Once again, the Steering Group has no positive proposal to make to deal with the obvious problems that the Law Commission was seeking to solve.

---

[117] See *Developing the Framework*, para. 4.103.

Index